HOW TO SURVIVE

How to Survive

The Extraordinary Resilience of Ordinary People

Andy Steiner

Think Piece Publishing | *Singular Voices. Social Issues.*
MINNEAPOLIS

ISBN: 978-0-9892352-5-9 (paperback)
ISBN: 978-0-9892352-6-6 (ePub)
ISBN: 978-0-9892352-7-3 (Kindle)

Printed in the United States of America
Designed by Mayfly Design and typeset in the Quadraat OT and Meta typefaces
First Printing: 2015

19 18 17 16 15   5 4 3 2 1

Think Piece Publishing
Singular Voices. Social Issues.
www.thinkpiecepublishing.com

To Alicia and Harry

Contents

Acknowledgments

I am inordinately thankful for the trusting kindness of the many people who shared their stories of everyday survival. Without them this book would not exist.

A long time ago, I told my friend Adam Wahlberg about a book I'd like to write. Later, after I had long given up on the project, Adam approached me to say that was leaving his job and starting his own company and that he would like to publish my book. I couldn't imagine a more eager, enthusiastic, or thoughtful publisher. My collaboration with Adam has been a lucky pleasure.

Years ago, when I first started working on this book, I sent an e-mail to friends and colleagues asking for suggestions of people I might want to profile in this book. Thanks to everyone who responded with sources, encouragement, and advice.

Throughout the long process of conceiving, reporting, and writing this book, I've sought the advice of many talented friends and former colleagues, including the amazing Cathy Madison and Jerry Creedon. Many thanks to both of you for your time, advice, and willing ears. I recall that Frank Bures added sharp insight, wit, and direction on this book's title. Thank you. A debt is owed to the Rev. Janne Eller-Isaacs, a knowledgeable early resource who added useful insight to my reporting. And a grateful nod goes to the great Jessica Gallo, who lent her skilled eye.

To my sweet, smart, sassy daughters, Astrid and Iris: thank you for your faith, encouragement, and support. And never-ending thanks is owed to my sweetheart, John.

Introduction
Our Fragile, Imperfect, Beautiful, Powerful Lives

This book isn't about me.

Or at least that's what I kept telling myself when I first embarked on this project. I'm trained as a journalist, so I donned my hat of objectivity and set out to locate and interview people who'd lived through trauma and defined themselves as survivors.

As my interviews started to pile up, it didn't take long for me to begin feeling the weight and the sadness and the truth and the joy in my subjects' stories. Then I began looking at the people around me a little bit more carefully. What I discovered was that bad things eventually happen to everyone, and that just about everyone holds some capacity to survive.

That's when I realized that this book really *was* about me—and also about everyone else on this planet.

One memory keeps coming back. Decades ago now, when I was in my mid-twenties, I was seriously ill and had to go to an urgent-care center. It was one of the lowest points of my then fairly short life. Sick, tired, and scared, I felt strangely comforted when a nurse lightly touched my shoulder and said, sweeping her hand in a gesture that seemed to take in everyone, patients and health care providers alike, "Welcome to the ranks of the walking wounded. You might not be able to recognize us at first glance, but we're everywhere."

I still clearly remember how she used the words "we" and "us," deftly including herself—and me—in the ranks. To be defined as a wounded person felt jarring, but somehow beautiful. I looked around that room and saw people of every color, age, and size. Some looked obviously sick, some healthy and vigorous. I had felt so alone in my own particular trauma that I couldn't see the traumas of others. When the busy nurse made her comment and then rushed off to help another patient, it was like my blinders were knocked off. The rest of the world—bright, confusing, noisy—suddenly filled my vision.

For a moment, anyhow, I didn't feel so alone—or, for that matter, so self-obsessed. Same goes for my work on this book. As my research deepened, and my interviews expanded, I felt a strange sense of peace and community within other people's stories of struggle. I felt wiser; comforted by the reality that trauma is something we all experience, something we all can survive.

So if you're still wondering: *What makes her qualified to write this book on survival?* Your answer is in the paragraphs you just read. Trauma is a shared human experience. I am a trained writer, a researcher, an interviewer, and an observer of the human condition. But, like everyone else on this planet, I am also a fragile human being. I have experienced my own traumas both big and small. Somehow I've survived them and gone on to live my own mostly quiet, mostly happy life. I've included my own experiences in this book when it felt appropriate, but mostly I've focused on other people's stories—because they always seem more interesting than my own. I'm working to turn my focus outward, rather than inward, to realize the connections and humanity created by the shared human experiences of trauma, resiliency, and survival.

By the end of this book, I hope you'll see the world the same way.

From victim to victor: The survivor's journey

Sometimes with very little warning—and often none at all—bad fortune rains down from the sky.

Father Michael Lapsley, a South African Anglican priest and anti-apartheid activist, discovered this reality one morning more than two decades ago when he opened a package sent from South Africa to his home in exile in Zimbabwe. Hidden between the pages of two religious magazines was a bomb. The blast blew off both of Lapsley's hands, destroyed one eye, and shattered his eardrums. Later, it was discovered that the bomb was sent by individuals opposed to Lapsley's human-rights work.

Recovering from the physical trauma was a long and arduous process—Lapsley spent months in an Australian rehabilitation center—but what he learned was that the process of *physical* survival, of helping his body heal from his injuries, was nothing compared with the strength it took to take the next step, to forgive his attacker and move on with his own life.

There is no doubt that Lapsley had been a victim of a horrible crime, but with time he refused to be defined by the violence that had been inflicted on him. Instead he chose to use the experience to inform his own life and positively affect the lives of others. To do that, he realized he had to move beyond the trauma.

"The imagery I often use is when something terrible has happened to you, you have one of two responses," Lapsley tells me. "One response is to say and believe, 'Something has been done to me.' In that response we say we are a victim. We may survive the trauma physically, but if we never move beyond that emotional sense of ourselves as a *victim*, we remain prisoners of that one moment in history. We are stuck there forever."

Lapsley takes a deep breath and continues.

"Think of life being like a river. The river flows unencumbered until this terrible thing happens, this thing that defines us as victim. When trauma happens, when we don't move on, we become a stone in the river. The water whirlpools over and around us, but we ourselves are stuck. We live only in terms of that moment in history." For Lapsley, the struggle seemed immense, but he was determined not to become a stone in the river.

In 1992, Lapsley returned to South Africa from Australia. "What I saw was a damaged nation," he recalls. "The damage had been done to our humanity by what we'd done, what had been done to us, and by what we'd failed to do. All South Africans had a story to tell. My story had been acknowledged and recognized, but for many survivors all they had was their victimhood. We were a nation of victims."

Within this realization was the seed of an idea. Lapsley saw that people in his adopted nation (born in Australia, he'd become a naturalized South African citizen in the mid-1970s) needed a way to move past the inertia created by trauma, to acknowledge past misdeeds and move forward. The post-apartheid Truth and Reconciliation Commission was born of this same impulse, as was Lapsley's own nonprofit, the Institute for Healing of Memories, an organization that works to contribute to the healing journey of individuals, communities, and nations.

As the organization's director, Lapsley travels the world speaking about his experiences and conducting workshops designed to help foster healing from trauma inflicted on individuals by wars, repressive regimes, human-rights abuses, and other traumatic events or circumstances. "What I talk about is the journey of becoming a victor," he says. "That's when the river starts to flow again. We no longer live life in terms of this terrible thing, no matter what that terrible thing might be. We move from object of history to subject of history."

Lapsley believes that he survived the horror that was inflicted upon him by resisting the all-too-human impulse to become just another stone in the river. He moved beyond the trauma, refusing to define himself by what had happened to him, and instead defining himself by what he could do to positively shape his own life and the lives of other human beings.

Inner strength

But perhaps Michael Lapsley and his resilient reaction to trauma is nothing more than an anomaly. Nan Henderson, a clinical social worker and co-founder and president of Resiliency In Action, a Santa Barbara, California–based consulting group that runs trainings, workshops, and classes on resiliency, doesn't think so.

She believes that nearly everyone in the world—no matter what their personal experience—holds the capacity for survival. In other words, no matter what challenges life dishes out, deep inside we all own the tools needed to survive. And we are born equipped with those tools.

Henderson didn't learn this perspective in school.

"I had been trained as a clinical social worker in the 1980s," she says. "I was working primarily with youth and their families. The youth that I worked with were struggling with substance abuse, school failure, mental-health issues, and violence. I had just earned my master's in clinical social work. Like everyone else, I was trained in what I like to call the 'deficit model.'"

Henderson says that the deficit model is a way of categorizing and diagnosing clients by focusing on the challenges in their life histories. During an intake session, a social worker trained in the deficit model will categorize clients through a battery of questions designed to assess the challenges that hold them back. Even from the earliest days of her career, Henderson had a hard time working from the deficit-model framework.

"I realized that focusing on what was *wrong* with kids did not motivate them to heal," she says. "It depressed them and their parents. It wasn't an empowering model. It made them feel like, in the face of great challenge, they were destined to fail. It didn't provide any kind of lifeline or uncover their strengths."

Henderson began searching the academic literature, looking for research that supported her belief that there had to be a better way to help and encourage children facing serious life challenges.

"In 1990, I discovered the concept of resiliency," she says. "Very few people were writing about the concept at that time, but what I saw felt really exciting. A group of renegade psychologists were rebelling against the deficit model. They were saying that people are more than their problems. You can't focus on what's wrong with people, they wrote: Everybody is a mixture of strengths and problems, and this reality has to be emphasized."

This realization was thrilling for Henderson. It opened up vistas of innate hope and strength that she had sensed for years but had never been able to articulate. "It was a huge epiphany in my career," she says.

Out of this epiphany grew Resiliency In Action, a partnership between Henderson and several colleagues. The group speaks to educators, health care providers, parents, and business owners about ways they can help build and encourage strength and resiliency in themselves and the people they serve.

"Ever since then, my work has been based on helping people discover their inner resilience—even people who face overwhelming trauma and challenge," Henderson tells me. "Once people recognize that flicker of resiliency in themselves and in others, it's just a small step to realizing the larger reality of the resilience that exists in everyone and everything in the world." It's a hopeful, empowering reality that Henderson believes is worth repeating.

Ordinary survivors, extraordinary survival

Trauma doesn't discriminate. When human beings experience traumatic events—no matter what the source—our reactions are similar. And we are given choices about what to make of those experiences. We all, no matter what our situation, have the option to clear the river, to rejoin the waters and continue on with life.

"We have a need as human beings to make sense of why bad things happen to us," Lapsley says. And it is important for all humans to understand that bad luck is blind, that there is no surefire way to protect oneself from trauma, especially trauma of the most everyday kind. "The longer we live, the more likely something bad will happen to us or somebody we love. In some ways we don't know how we will respond to trauma until it happens to us. This reality—or this core sense of life's unpredictability—involves the totality of us as human beings. It involves us spiritually, psychologically, emotionally."

It is life, Lapsley says, and it is the life we have been given to live. Our time on this earth is limited, and we have the power to make the most out of everything that happens—good or bad, uplifting or traumatic.

We are all just one step away from having the rug pulled out from under our feet. Our lives, our happiness, our sense of well-being is really that fragile. That realization can feel frightening, but if you take a slow, steady breath and parse it down, maybe understanding that everyone on this earth—like everyone in that long-ago urgent-care center—is a fragile being, that the veil that divides trauma and everyday happiness is thin and permeable, could also provide you with a curious sense of freedom and humanity.

I've understood that truth as a *concept* for some time, but try as I might, some days that doesn't make it any easier to accept. I buy insurance, write a will, practice my little superstitions. But I'm working on it. I try to focus on what's happening now and not worry about the future or fixate on the past. I'm working toward a feeling of peace with the universe's unknowns, a sense of confidence that I hold the inner strength needed to help me survive trauma.

This book—and the people it describes—are helping me get there. I hope they help you get there, too.

Chapter 1
How to Survive a Heart Attack

Picture me, in my doctor's office, hooked up to an ECG machine. I'm embarrassed, a little bit tearful, even. To make matters worse, the tears make me feel embarrassed, too, so I'm a mess, really, sniffly and sheepish, trying to explain to the kind doctor, and then to her nurse, as she's sticking probes to my chest, "I'm writing this book and I'm interviewing a youngish woman who had a heart attack. She's really fit, around my age, a marathoner, but she *had a heart attack*, and her symptoms weren't typical at all. Now I keep thinking I'm having one, too . . ." my words fade off.

I'm making a ridiculous scene, and when my ECG results come back normal, as in "You are not having a heart attack, Idiot," instead of feeling relieved, I actually feel even more embarrassed, if that's possible. I blow my nose, quickly thank the doctor for her time, and slink out of the clinic, feeling like I am wearing a scarlet **H** for hypochondriac.

Later, when I meet up with Jen, The Healthy Youngish Woman Who Had A Heart Attack, and tell her my story, I steel myself for her reaction. And it's not the cynical, scoffing response I'd feared.

"People tell me different versions of that same story all the time," Jen says, kindly. She's a fit, compact former gymnast, a reserved-yet-friendly woman with a neatly side-parted short, blonde haircut, intelligent eyes, and a ready smile. She lives with her husband and two sons in St. Paul. She laughs lightly and says, "My yoga teacher just told me that one day she was driving home and was so convinced that *she* was having a heart attack that she drove herself to the emergency room. She'd heard my story and she was feeling really aware of symptoms." At the ER, medical staff examined Jen's yoga instructor and assured her that her heart was just fine.

Like me, the yoga instructor was embarrassed by all the attention, but Jen says that when it comes to heart health, it's best to push embarrassment aside. "Sure, when you're focused on it, every little twinge might feel like you're about to die," Jen says, "but so many people—women especially—avoid seeking medical attention for a heart attack until it is too late." That's partially why the fatality rate for heart disease is so high. "If you're concerned about your heart, you should get it checked out and not feel like a fool for doing it."

One Sunday morning three years ago, Jen felt a bit foolish when she drove herself to the emergency room for what she figured was a severe case of reflux. The then-37-year-old mother of two had been up most of the night with what felt like the worst heartburn she'd ever experienced. For a few days before, she'd felt pain between her shoulder blades while running, but it would eventually go away. She'd also been feeling more easily fatigued, but she blamed it on not eating enough food to fuel her through her grueling workouts.

Jen was, after all, in what she thought was the best shape of her life. She'd already run one marathon and was months away from her second. She was at a healthy weight, having shed the extra pounds she'd gained while pregnant with her second child. She was working to improve her—and her family's—diet. Her cholesterol, which had been significantly high for most of her life, seemed to be coming down incrementally. ("My highest number ever was 383 when I was in my 20s," Jen tells me, shaking her head. "I was on a cholesterol drug briefly then, but, because it took so long for me to get pregnant, and I didn't want to be on them when I was trying, I had been off the meds for years. At the time of my heart attack, my cholesterol was down to 230.") The year before, Jen had stepped away from her high-stress job to spend time at home with her children. She was also fighting stress with yoga, feeling so inspired by the practice that she fantasized about becoming a yoga instructor someday.

But then there was the heart attack.

"I had been training for the marathon all summer," Jen says. "In retrospect, I knew I was slowing down. Running was getting harder for me, but I was trying to ignore it. The week of my heart attack, I ran 17 miles, but I had to sit down after eight, because I was feeling so dizzy. I just thought I hadn't eaten enough."

Another sign was when she got on her bike. The super-achieving Jen was also training for a duathlon, and when she went on a training ride the day before her heart attack, she had to quit less than halfway through. "It hurt like hell," she says now. Jen even made a point of telling her husband, Scott—her grade-school friend and high-school and college sweetheart—about the pain. "I said to him, 'I have this weird pain in my back and it sometimes goes down my arm. I feel like you should know that.'"

That evening, Jen went out for spicy Thai food with a friend. When she got home, the pain intensified. At first, she blamed the pain on the food.

"I thought, 'I shouldn't have ordered it so spicy,'" Jen says. "Then I went to bed, and when I lay down it was like someone took a knife and twisted it in the middle of my back. The pain went down both shoulders and down my arms. I thought it must be heartburn. But it was worse than any heartburn I'd ever felt."

Jen had suffered from acid reflux before, and this pain felt different. Around one in the morning, she got out of bed and began Googling "reflux and back pain."

"I found a bunch of articles that said that combination of symptoms is normal," Jen says. "So I took six Advil and propped myself up with pillows and tried to sleep. I just wanted the ache in my arms to go away. Eventually I fell asleep for a bit, but the pain still didn't go away. I went back to Dr. Google and found something that said, 'If you read something that says reflux and arm pain is normal, that's baloney. It is a heart attack.'"

Frightened, Jen started researching heart-attack symptoms. She found a list that included upper-back and shoulder pain (check), stomach pain (check), anxiety (check). Jen had yet to experience one common heart-attack symptom on the list—breaking into a cold sweat.

"Then, just as I'm sitting at the computer, reading about that symptom," she says, still incredulous at the memory, "I am suddenly drenched in this cold sweat."

When Jen's husband woke, she told him that she'd been up sick most of the night. They had planned to drive their eldest son to his first sleep-away camp that morning, but Jen said she thought she should go to the doctor instead. Scott would plan on driving both children to the camp drop-off, but if Jen was done with the doctor soon enough, she'd join them. She promised to call his cell phone with updates. Because it was a Sunday morning and her doctor's office was closed, Jen would have to go to the emergency room.

The pain was stronger than ever, but Jen still helped her son pack for camp. After her family left, she took a shower, dried her hair and even put on makeup. "I was worried that there was something serious going wrong with me but I also told myself that in the end, the doctors would say it was nothing," she tells me. "I figured they were probably going to send me home."

When Jen got to the emergency room, she reported that she was experiencing back and arm pain and that she suspected it could be reflux, a condition she'd experienced before. She also said that one relative—her father—had heart disease. (He'd had hardening of the arteries in his fifties and had been given a stent, but never had an actual heart attack.) Then she sat down to wait (and wait) to see a doctor.

Because Jen now knows just about everything there is to know about heart disease and women, she sees her story as sadly typical. "Too often, that's how it goes with women," she sighs. "What do women do when they are having a heart attack? They put on their makeup first. They wait in line patiently. I consider myself a feminist, but when I was in the hospital having a heart attack, I just sat there patiently." She throws her hands up in the air.

Women's heart attack symptoms are often different than men's. But until recently, more typical symptoms of heart attack in women—nausea, back and neck pain, influenza-like body aches—were rarely mentioned in medical literature. That's likely because research has historically been based on male subjects. "Everyone expects a person having a heart attack to have chest pains, to clutch their chest and fall to the floor," Jen says, "but my heart attack never presented itself that way."

Jennifer Dankle is a cardiologist and even she didn't realize when her seventy-something mother was having a heart attack.

"My mom had a viral illness that was quite severe, and she was hospitalized for over a week," Dankle, a physician at the University of Minnesota, told me. At the time of her mother's heart attack, Dankle was in the final years of her residency. "Because she had a heart-rhythm disorder related to her viral illness, after she was released from the hospital, my mom was scheduled for a follow-up visit with a cardiologist. Mom complained of pain in the back of her neck. I didn't think much of it. But when the cardiologist gave her an ECG in his office, he discovered that she was having a heart attack right then." Dankle lets out an irritated sigh. "I thought I was pretty smart, and all along my mom was having a heart attack right in front of me. I didn't pick up on it."

Since going into practice, Dankle has seen several female patients with medical histories similar to Jen's. Most didn't recognize the symptoms they were experiencing as heart related. And many medical professionals didn't, either.

"We don't know much about women and heart disease," she sighs. "We have to shift the focus, it's clear. Since 1987, more women than men have died of heart disease, but of all the studies we've done, the vast majority have been on men. We don't have good research or data about how heart disease presents in women. We also don't have good treatments developed that are tailored specifically to women."

A new normal

It took emergency-room doctors ten hours to diagnose Jen's heart attack. At first, they said that her pain originated from a pinched nerve. A nurse performed an ECG, and the results were normal. Jen's blood was drawn and sent to the lab for analysis. The results were interesting: Jen's troponin enzyme levels were elevated, a known marker of heart attack. But distance runners are also sometimes known to have elevated troponin levels, and this—combined with Jen's age and general good health—steered doctors away from diagnosing myocardial infarction—medical-speak for heart attack.

There was even talk of discharge, of sending Jen home with pain medication for her back, but something told her to refuse.

"At this point, my husband was on his way to camp with the boys," Jen says, gritting her teeth. She's telling me this story at a quiet table in a comfortable coffee shop just blocks away from her house, and though she's recounted the tale many times before, she still appears shaken by the memory. "Scott had no idea what was going on. The last time I had called him was a few hours into the emergency-room visit and I had said, 'They didn't know what was wrong with me but they just gave me nitroglycerine.' All I knew was that the longer I was in the ER, the worse I felt."

Eventually, doctors agreed to admit Jen to a room in the hospital, though they still did not feel that her problem originated in her heart. But when she described her pain to an admitting nurse, things suddenly began to speed up.

"I told her, 'I'm an athlete. I know what muscle pain feels like and it isn't muscle pain. It hurts worse than childbirth.'" At this point, Jen says she had a feeling that her pain was originating from somewhere deep inside her body. She asked the nurse, "If I said it was chest pain, would they move any faster?" The nurse found a cardiologist who, theorizing that Jen may be suffering from a liver disorder sometimes found in distance athletes, agreed to perform an angiogram, a test in which a physician threads a thin, flexible catheter through a patient's groin and injects a liquid dye that highlights coronary blockages and other potentially fatal heart conditions.

"At this point I was in a lot of pain and it was getting worse all the time," Jen tells me, her eyes welling. "I said, 'Just fix it. I don't care anymore. Just make the pain go away.'"

During the angiogram, it was confirmed that Jen was, indeed, experiencing a heart attack. She had 100 percent blockage in one of her arteries and partial blockage in two others. Doctors cleared the major block and inserted a drug-emitting stent. She was prescribed medication to help control her cholesterol and keep the other blockages from growing.

For many people, a heart attack creates scar tissue in the heart that makes recovery difficult and can lead to lifelong disability. But Jen's case was different. Her cardiologist explained that her heart had been strengthened by all of her running, and remarkably, she emerged from a major attack with a heart that was scar-free. While recovery was going to be difficult, the doctor told Jen that she would have an easier time than most.

"My husband said, 'It turns out you weren't training for a marathon. You were actually training for a heart attack.'" Jen says. Her workouts had strengthened her heart and—in a perverse way—helped her notice that something was going wrong. Even better, because she was young and healthy, Jen's cardiologist gave her permission to train for another marathon as soon as she gave her body time to recover from this event.

Jen told herself that her heart attack was a blip in her personal history, a one-time event that she could box up and store safely in the past. But that didn't make it easy for Jen to accept the fact that her body—something she'd spent much of her life building up and strengthening—had seriously malfunctioned.

"At first, I was in denial. It was like, 'No, this is not happening,'" Jen says. "It probably took twenty-four hours after the heart attack, when I was recovering in the ICU, for the reality of what had just happened to really sink in," she says. "I was still e-mailing people about a work project from my phone while I was in an ICU bed. It took about a day post-surgery to let go of that old reality." Jen stayed in the hospital for three more days.

"I was numb," she says. "I was scatterbrained. I couldn't focus. I know now it was depression. I couldn't make a decision. Even when I was out of the hospital, I felt like I was watching myself from the outside. It was like I was not me anymore."

Depression is common among people who have had a heart attack, says Russell Luepker, MD, Mayo professor of public health at the University of Minnesota School of Public Health. Part of the depression is purely situational, he says. "Someone who thought they were healthy and doing fine suddenly discovers that they have a lifetime illness." Other post-heart-attack depression is chemical.

"Some of the drugs—including beta-blockers—that we give people who've had a heart attack tend to make them feel more tired," he says. "That wiped-out feeling can make a person feel depressed."

Steve Smalley, a cardiologist at Regions Hospital in St. Paul, says the correlation between heart disease and depression is too big to ignore. Cardiologists and their patients need to face this reality and monitor for it as routine practice following a cardiac event.

"Fifty percent of people will experience some form of depression after having a heart attack," Smalley tells me. "And untreated depression is correlated to a worse outcome for patients. It's important to treat this aspect of the disease."

By far the biggest obstacle that Jen faced was the realization that, far from being a distant memory she could shove away in a dusty corner of her past, her heart disease was something that she was going to have to face every day. There were the mountains of pills she was required to take. There was the twelve-week hospital rehab program she was required to attend. There were the nights she lay in bed, afraid to go to sleep, wondering if she would be woken by a mysterious ache or pain.

"It did not take me long to understand that once you have a heart attack, you have heart disease and you have it forever," Jen says. "This is not a one-time dramatic, traumatic event that is kind of interesting later. I was now a person with heart disease, a chronic illness. I struggled with that new identity right away."

Jen was clearly feeling wiped out and depressed. Her husband saw it. So did her family and friends. She tried toughing it out for a couple of months, thinking that as her heart improved so would her mood. But it didn't, and at the urging of her cardiologist, Jen added an antidepressant to her medication. "It was a very good decision," she says now.

Scott, Jen's husband, tells me he understands why Jen felt alone, sad, and frightened. "It makes complete sense to me. There you are, living your normal life and this big, scary, life-threatening thing happens to you. Suddenly other people can't relate to you. All you've got is yourself."

Somebody out there

Because, as an outwardly healthy 37-year-old woman, Jen didn't fit the description of a typical heart-attack patient, it was hard for her to find others to relate to. Part of the rehab program at her hospital included a support group. Jen attended faithfully, but she never felt like she fit in.

"When I started, there was one woman and four men in my group and everybody was a couple of decades older than me," Jen says. "By the time I left, the group was half women and half men but they were still all older. On the second day, this guy I call Tall Patrick leaned over and said to me, 'What are you doing here? You didn't have surgery, did you?'" She laughs at the memory. "I just didn't fit the profile."

By trade, Jen is a writer and communicator. So when she was faced with the reality of her heart attack, her first impulse was to write and communicate.

While she was still in the hospital recovering from her heart attack, Jen opened up her laptop and started writing about what happened. Jen is friendly and open, but she's also a little bit introverted, and too much talking can feel exhausting. She wanted to send a message to friends and family about what had happened and the steps she was taking to improve her health. Her first message was a Facebook post from her hospital bed, but it quickly grew. "I was just tired of being on the phone, telling everybody what happened," she says. Later, Jen abandoned Facebook for her own blog.

"I started the heart blog to process my emotions and keep track of what I was learning," she says. "I wanted to know about how I could protect myself. I wanted to know why I was the only one in three generations in my family to have a heart attack. My grandfather didn't have a heart attack. My grandmother has heart disease. So does my father. But nobody but me had had a heart attack. I thought, 'Why me? I'm 37 and I was running. Why didn't they have one?' I was doing a lot of research and reading a ton. I wanted to keep track of everything."

At first, Scott believes that the blog was a way for Jen to avoid talking about her health. "She's not the type of person that at a big family gathering wants some relative to come up to her and say"—he adopts an annoying sad-sack voice—"'How are you doing? Let's talk about your disease.' The blog ended up being a way to communicate to people how she's doing without having to call everyone up on the phone or [having them] come visit, kind of like a Caring Bridge site. Then it started ballooning into the advocacy."

Jen quickly saw that her writing was helping others. That felt like an important validation. "The blog wasn't up very long before somebody found me and wrote in the middle of the night, 'My husband who's 37 just had a heart attack and I'm here trying to find out how we are going to go forward and I found you.' Then other people, young women with heart disease especially, found me and started writing. And suddenly there was another reason I was doing all that writing." In helping others, Jen helped herself. She had created her own support group.

As Jen's blogging intensified, so did her interest in heart-health activism. When she learned that her state's Heart Association was seeking spokeswomen for their Go Red for Women campaign, Jen decided to audition for the role. Putting herself out there wasn't typical behavior; before the heart attack, Jen generally preferred a behind-the-scenes role. But this felt different. One Saturday, several months after her heart attack, Jen drove herself to a casting call at the Mall of America.

"I didn't tell anyone else but my husband I was going," Jen recalls. "But for some reason I just thought, 'I'm going to go try this.' My interview went well. I cried. I made the interviewer cry. Then I left, and three months later I get an email from the American Heart Association telling me that I was the 2013 Minnesota winner of the casting call."

As part of her job as a spokesperson, Jen maintains a Heart Association website (www.mylifeinred.net) and appears as a featured speaker at heart-health awareness events around the state. She has to tell her story over and over (and over) again, but for now, at least, she doesn't mind. In fact, she says, the work helps give her life focus and direction. Every time she tells the story of the night she nearly died, Jen reminds herself that she is a survivor.

"I guess I really can say my heart is on my sleeve," Jen laughs, rolling her eyes at her own bad pun. "At first, I wondered when I started the blog, 'Will I stop? Will I get bored? Will I eventually have nothing left to say?' It's been more than a year and I still find something to say, not with the frequency that I did at first, but still pretty often. And then when I became a spokesperson, all the activism just moved to a different level. I don't feel like my heart attack defines me, but it's OK if it is part of my identity. To me there's a difference."

One step forward. Two steps back.

Saying that Jen feels well served by her doctor is putting it lightly.

"He's great, amazing," she says of Bilal Murad, MD. He was on duty the night of her heart attack, but she only met him when he was called in to perform her emergency angiogram. "I love him. He's different than other doctors, more involved, more responsive. I feel like he's really on my side."

Beyond the fact that he likely saved her life that night, Murad won Jen's devotion with his focus on helping her live as normal a life post-heart-attack as possible.

"His philosophy is, 'You are young. Let's live your life. It's ridiculous not to do things,'" she says. "Every time I have an appointment, he draws an anatomical heart and says for me what's going on in my heart. The first time he did that he flipped over the paper and wrote down his email and his cell phone number. He said that I can contact him at any time. I cried on the spot. No doctor does that."

For Jen, part of living her life was having a third child. She and her husband hoped to try for another soon, but she couldn't get pregnant while taking her mountain of pills. After Jen successfully completed eight weeks of outpatient rehab and passed several stress tests, Murad gave her the clear to return to life as before. This included marathon running and baby making.

"He said, 'You are healthy. Go back to your life,'" Jen says. "He even said, 'If you want to have a baby, I'll let you. I want you to live your life. You're not 80. You're 37.'"

For the time being, Jen set the idea of another baby to the side and focused on a more immediate goal. The marathon she had been training for when she had her first heart attack would be held again in October, and she set her eyes on the goal of running it again.

"I ran shorter distances in the spring," Jen says. "I ran a marathon relay in May. Then I had another round of tests and got final permission to run the marathon."

At the beginning, Jen's husband, Scott, felt anxious about her running post-heart-attack. So he started running with her. "I wanted to be near her," he says. "I thought if something's going to happen to her while she was running, I wanted to be there." After Jen passed the medical tests, Scott felt more reassured that she'd be OK, and she started to run by herself again during the day while the kids were in school.

"Even after she'd done many, many runs by herself, I'd still ask her to text me when she leaves and text me when she gets back," Scott tells me. He's a smart, kind, soft-spoken, bespectacled man. "If Jen was gone longer than I thought her run should take, I would get anxious. I'd think, 'She should be done by now,'" he pauses to control his emotions. "But she always got back. You eventually realize that anything could happen at any time. You can't let worry or 'what ifs' take over your life."

I'd like to close this chapter with the triumphant image of Jen crossing the marathon finish line, throwing her arms skyward, and signaling the end of her long and exhausting journey with heart disease. But, like most people's, Jen's doesn't wrap up neatly.

She continued to train for the marathon all summer, going on regular runs. But by August, she could tell that something was wrong.

"I tried to ignore it at first," Jen tells me. "In late August, when I was running, I started to feel that little pain between my shoulder blades again. It happened only when I ran, and it would go away after about a mile. For some crazy reason, I wasn't positive it was a heart-attack-related pain. Even though it felt about the same as it had the first time, I kept telling myself, 'I'm crazy. It's in my head.' I just didn't know how to listen to my body anymore."

Despite her doubts, Jen kept running—and questioning. "I'd monitor the pain and for a while it would go away," she says. "I did notice that I was slowing down. I remembered that had happened last year, too, before my heart attack. Still, I thought, 'This can't be happening again.' No matter how hard I tried, my pace was slower, not better. I was feeling out of fuel. The last time, before my heart attack, I always thought that slowness was about food. But it turns out it is really about oxygen."

While Jen was spending her time debating whether her heart was malfunctioning, she got a call from her 32-year-old brother, Mike. He was in an ambulance on his way to the hospital. He had just had a heart attack.

For nearly a week before his heart attack, Mike, a married father of four who owns a cabinet-making business in northern Minnesota, had been feeling sluggish. Also a marathoner, he had noticed that he felt short of breath when he was on training runs. Then there were the "heartburn-y chest pains," Mike recalls. "They were nothing like you see in the movies—some guy clutching his chest and falling down. They'd come and go, so I didn't worry about them too much." Turns out, Mike's "heartburn" was actually angina, chest pain or discomfort a person feels when their heart muscle is not getting enough blood.

Like Jen, the night before he went to the hospital with a heart attack, Mike was up for an hour or two with what he figured was a bad case of heartburn. Like his sister before him, he "took a couple of ibuprofen, had a glass of water, looked up some symptoms on the Internet, but they went away, so I went back to bed." In the morning the pain was back, and Mike went to the doctor. Things were feeling serious.

"It was hurting so bad that I arrived at 9:30, half an hour early for my appointment," Mike says. "I walked into the waiting room. I said, 'I'm having chest pains. I have to sit down.' In ten seconds, they had me in the back room. My doctor knows about Jenny's heart attack. He was my dad's doctor, too. In what felt like ten minutes, they threw me in an ambulance and sent me to the hospital in Fargo. By one in the afternoon, my angioplasty was finished and I was in the recovery room."

When Jen heard what had happened to Mike she fell apart. "He had said, 'I have this pain in my back' when we went for a run a few weeks before," she says. "When I get this call from the ambulance going to the hospital, I just literally fell on the floor. It was not a proportional response, I know, but I felt like all that I did, all of the research and the writing and talking about heart health, didn't help. My little brother still had a heart attack. The next thought I had was, honestly, about myself. I thought, 'I'm never going to be better. I'm never going to be well.'"

Jen rushed to Fargo to help her brother and his family. Even from his hospital bed, Mike could see that Jen wasn't handling this latest development well.

"My heart attack made Jen numb and mentally checked out," Mike tells me. While the fact that he had just had a heart attack made Mike feel uneasy, he had a more matter-of-fact reaction to the news. He knew he had a family history of heart disease. He knew he had high cholesterol and had been on and off cholesterol medication since he was fourteen.

Mike loves and respects his older sister. In fact, since her heart attack—and even more since his—he's joked that the two of them are members of what he likes to call "The Heart-Attack Club." Jen and Mike also have one other sister, spaced between them. She has not suffered from heart problems and tries to avoid the conversation. Mike thinks it's her way of avoiding the inevitable.

"Everybody responds to things like this differently," he says. "I don't respond to life as emotionally as Jen does, but I don't try to ignore reality, either." Jen is a thinker, a ruminator, Mike tells me. He is less inclined to spend too much time trying to predict the future.

"They tell you there are five major risk factors for heart disease: smoking, family history, weight, diet, and exercise. Those are the five things you can do something about. I can't do anything about my genes. I figure you do what you can do and not worry about the rest of it. There's nothing you can do about it."

Steve Smalley says he's seen patients take many different approaches to coping with the reality of chronic illness after a heart attack. "The people who do the best are ones who have the philosophy that they are not their disease. Somehow, they manage to separate themselves from the disease. They believe they are people with a condition and they are going to manage that condition like they are going to manage everything else in their lives. Many have a larger philosophy or guiding force in their lives that helps them rise above the trauma of their health issues. They see that there is something else out there that they can focus their energies on."

Part of survival after heart attack is about attitude and perspective, which can be hard won, Smalley says. "Successful patients live one day at a time and they don't worry about six months from now or two years from now. They adopt the 'I'm here today. I'm dealing with this today' attitude." Another approach that Smalley has seen to be successful is closer to Jen's.

"These patients become very proactive," he says. "They might come to an appointment and say they've been online, or they've talked to other people about heart disease. They are self-starters. They are motivated." But both approaches have a common theme, Smalley adds. "Instead of waiting to see what the disease gives them next, the people who really thrive are the ones who adapt around it. They move on. They want to have a full life no matter what hits them. They have this way of not being their disease."

Mike knows just what the doctor is talking about. "People get weirded out when they hear I've had a heart attack," he says. "They like to tell themselves it is a once-in-a-lifetime event. But the truth is I am statistically likely to have more heart attacks. That's a little crazy. But once I got my mind wrapped around that fact and understood what to do about it, it helped me relax."

He also credits his older sister's writing and research with helping him feel prepared for what was coming after his own heart attack. "Jenny's writing about her experience raised my awareness about everything," he says. "It was almost like it was easier for me to have my heart attack because none of it was new to me. I was like, 'Yeah, yeah, yeah. I got this,' because I had heard it all from her. I knew what to expect."

Here we go again

Three weeks after her brother's heart attack, Jen realized that she could no longer ignore the warning messages her heart was sending.

One beautiful weekend morning, she went out for a run and the pain between her shoulder blades fired up again. It was more than a dull ache this time. It was sharp and insistent.

"I hadn't even run a mile and it started to hurt. Bad," she says. "I knew then it was for real. It was acute pain. It felt like someone had put a knife in the middle of my back and twisted it. It had been a little twinge before, a hitch, but it was much, much worse this time. I had to walk home."

For this run, Jen had chosen a busy, popular route. "I was trying to walk where there were no people because I was crying," she says. "I didn't want anyone to see me. I knew then that I was done. I didn't need any tests. I just knew, 'I'm not running this marathon. In fact, I'm not running any marathon ever again.'"

The next day, Jen called her doctor's office. She went in for tests and eventually was told to schedule another angioplasty. During the procedure, Murad discovered a 75 percent blockage in Jen's left anterior descending artery, or LAD. The LAD is often referred to as "the widow maker," because if it is abruptly and completely blocked it will cause a massive heart attack that will likely lead to sudden death.

"Only five percent of people who have a heart attack in their LAD live," Jen says. "Because I was a runner, I diagnosed myself before I actually *had* a heart attack. My heart didn't hurt if I wasn't running."

During the angioplasty, Jen's cardiologist cleared out her LAD ("They use something like a Roto-Rooter," she jokes) and inserted a second drug-emitting stent. The next time I see Jen, it is just a little bit over a week since the procedure, and her chest is sore. She says that the "Roto-Rooter" angioplasty took longer and feels like it was more "thorough" than her first, and now she has pain that feels, disconcertingly, like a heart attack. She's feeling discouraged and set back, and I can see it clearly in her face and the slumped-in way she holds her body. Jen used to tell herself that her first heart attack was a fluke. Now she knows that she will have to monitor her heart for the rest of her life.

"The same doctor who said, 'I want you to live your life' now has changed his tune," Jen tells me. "He said, 'No more marathons for you,' and 'You're not going to have any more kids.' He also said,

'You're never going off these drugs,' and even, 'Here are some more and higher doses.'"

When her artery clogged for the second time, Jen knew she would never have another child. But it still hurt to hear her doctor say it. She realized that she had to accept the fact that she will never be free of heart disease, never be able to put the experience behind her. She realizes that for the rest of her life, she will have to take medicine, visit doctors, monitor her heart.

"Pregnancy is the ultimate stress test," Jen says, adding that she and her husband struggled for years to conceive their first son, who was born prematurely. It took several more years—and medical intervention—to conceive their second son. "It is harder on your heart than anything. The doctor said, 'Your heart can't handle it. You already have two kids who need you. You can't put your life at risk that way.' So I had to give that up, but it was very hard. Chronic illness of any kind takes away things you want. You have no choice but to give them up. I'm still adjusting to that reality."

Not like she planned it

Fit from his training runs by her side, Jen's husband finished the marathon. She watched from the sidelines with their sons. "On the day of the marathon, my doctor called me and said, 'I'm sorry you didn't get to do it,'" she says. "What made me sad that day was watching the older women run by looking so strong and proud. I intended to be that woman someday."

She sighs, and runs her hand through her hair. "What I once considered a one-time health crisis turned into a chronic illness," she says. Her future, as she now sees it, consists of a "stent every year until I'm 60, and then a quadruple bypass."

That future sounds bleak to Jen, and she tells herself that she is going to have to change the way she sees the world if she is going to be happy in the life she has been given. For anyone, changing the way you look at the world is a challenge; for the high-achieving, driven, focused Jen, adjusting her self-identity is a challenge. Before the heart attack, before children, she'd mapped out a future for herself and Scott. Jen realizes now that her map was drawn too early, before the geography of her life was fully developed.

Instead, a greater reality is now making itself clear to Jen, and that reality can be painful at times: The future can't be mapped. Life is beyond our control and no one is immune to trauma or tragedy.

Jen and Scott got a crash course in life's unpredictability after the birth of their first child. During her pregnancy, Jen developed a dangerous condition known as HELLP Syndrome, and their son was born two months prematurely. He had to stay in the NICU for many weeks.

"After my son was born, when I was driving my car or eating in a restaurant I'd look at other people going about their normal life, and I'd think, 'How are you able to do that? Don't you know the world is ending?'" Jen says. "Then, slowly, I began to realize that everyone I see has something hard in their lives. Very few people don't have some tragedy or some crisis that happens to them. And if they haven't yet, they will. Back then, it helped me to realize that I wasn't alone in this reality."

Now Jen knows that she has to use the strength she gained from watching her baby fight for his life to set her own life back on course. She's like a young bird that's mistakenly flown into a picture window, pausing to clear the bells from her head before righting herself and flying away.

"I've been completely brought to my knees before," Jen says to me, her hands spread open on the table between us. "Those were times where I could do nothing and I needed people to help me. I got through those times by asking for help, by accepting I was not in control and letting life take over for a moment." She takes a breath and continues, a bit of sadness creeping in around the corners of her eyes. "Letting go is hard work. For a person like me, it can be really exhausting."

Witnessing Jen struggling to pull her life back together has been difficult for Scott. "As her husband, it is hard to watch her try to work things out," he says. "I try to find little ways that I can help. But I think it's just going to take time and experience. It's like when your children are young and they are struggling to learn a new skill. It's hard to watch and do nothing, but you realize that you can only do so much for them or they'll never learn to do it themselves. You can't live that journey for them."

And, Scott asserts, Jen is no child. She's a strong, determined woman who faces life's challenges honestly and openly. Getting up after being knocked down isn't always pretty, but he'll always be there to offer a helping hand—if she needs it.

"The heart attack, I think, is by far the toughest thing Jen has had to deal with," Scott tells me. "She's been scared and sad but I've never seen her be anything close to giving up. Does she always have the most positive, great attitude? No. And I don't expect that. Still, she's strong. You might not always see her strong side right away, but it always comes out eventually."

Jen, Scott believes, is naturally wired to be a survivor.

"Both sides of her extended family are very positive, strong people with a can-do attitude," he says. "She's a firstborn who is very strong and confident. She has a strong foundation. She thinks, 'If I want to do something, I'm going to do it.' And she does it. She's that strong."

Fit as a fiddle

I don't think I'd like to spend a lot of time in the place where I almost died. But when Jen and I walk into the hospital where she had her heart attack, she's breezy, happy, relaxed—almost like she's visiting her neighborhood grocery store and chatting up the cashiers.

It's been almost two months since she had a second stent inserted in her heart, and the Jen I see today looks healthier, happier, and more confident than the subdued, still-aching woman I last saw. Jen's Hospital, as I've come to think of it, is a busy place, a bustling urban hospital with an emergency room that serves thousands of patients a month. It's snowy and cold outside, but inside Jen is smiling and relaxed, joking familiarly with staff and efficiently guiding me down halls toward the Heart and Vascular Care unit.

As we tour the unit, I ask Jen, "Does being here make you feel uneasy?" She thinks about my question for a minute and then shakes her head, saying, "I don't have bad associations with this place at all because rehab was so good for me. They saved my life here." Then we're right outside the room where Dr. Murad performed her angioplasties. Jen says, brightly, "Here's where they told my husband as I was being wheeled in for surgery, 'This is the kissing place. You have to kiss her here and then you have to leave.'"

Scott isn't nearly as fond of the hospital. "My husband doesn't like coming here. There are too many memories here for him. But for me, I walked in thinking, 'I'm going here to get fixed up,' and eventually they did fix me up."

Next, we visit the rehab center, where Jen completed the outpatient program after her heart attack. The crowded room is filled with monitors, treadmills, weights, and other exercise equipment. This is where Jen, the proud athlete and distance runner, faced some of the greatest physical challenges of her life.

By way of illustration, she points to a small set of stairs with a railing. "After my heart attack, going up and down these six steps was really hard," Jen says.

This morning, a lone patient is in the room, moving slowly and silently through a set of exercises. Jen recalls feeling the same way. "I'd be winded, exhausted just going up those few stairs. It took an amazing amount of effort. But I started feeling stronger after about a week. As time went on, I'd come in for my session and they'd say, 'You can only go this fast and you can only get your heart rate up a certain amount.'" Patients wear monitors while they work out, so staff can check their heart rates to make sure they are exercising safely. "They'd monitor me, and when I really started getting into it they'd say, 'Jen, slow down.' Eventually they gave me my own program because I was in better shape than some of the other patients. I was allowed to go faster on the treadmill for longer and I was allowed to skip some rotations to do harder work."

That measureable sense of improvement, of her body growing from weak to strong, helped boost Jen's confidence. The same is true today. Her heart is getting stronger. Her body is healing, and she has proof of that every time she runs on a treadmill or lifts a weight. Jen takes me across the street to ExerCare Fitness Center, a special medical gym where patients, staff, and community members can exercise in a medically supervised environment. The gym is staffed by nurses and exercise physiologists, so people who've had a heart attack, a stroke, or another medical issue can be assured that they will be safe while breaking a sweat. But you don't have to be a patient to join this gym. Jen says that other folks just like coming here because it's clean, well staffed, and full of high-tech workout equipment.

After her heart attack, Jen started working out at ExerCare. When she saw how good it felt to challenge her body again, she bit the bullet and signed up for several sessions with a personal trainer. After that concentrated time at the gym, Jen felt healed and ready to take on the world. Then her LAD got clogged up, and she had to start over again.

For nearly a month after this downturn, Jen avoided the gym. But the break was hard on her. She was sad, frustrated, and angry, and she missed the confidence that came with a strong body. Before her LAD clogged, she'd been training for another marathon, and now she was back to baby steps. Depressed and discouraged, she kept a low profile, avoiding the gym and the hospital—but she couldn't stay invisible for long.

Remember Tall Patrick from support group? "I see him all the time," Jen says, rolling her eyes. For a week or so it felt like she couldn't leave the house without running into him. "I'd see him at the grocery store, in the bank, at the pharmacy. Then he finally busted me at Starbucks. He said, 'I noticed that you haven't been at the gym. I'm going to tell them that I saw you and you're alive.'" Word got out that Jen was alive—but not kicking. "My old trainer sent me an email saying, 'Where are you? You should come in again,'" she says. "I'm thankful they didn't give up on me. It forced me to be accountable and get in here and exercise, which helps me a lot."

At ExerCare, Jen changes into her workout clothes and hops on the treadmill. Dr. Murad has told her that even though there will be no marathons in her future, she can still run shorter distances. This news was expected, but it still felt disappointing. Still, Jen's not giving up. It just means that she'll have to readjust her definition of fitness.

"I'm not going to stop running," Jen insists, keeping a good pace on the treadmill. "It's my diagnostic tool. It saved my life. Now that

I'm limited as to how far I can go, it will be hard for me to get as much satisfaction out of running as I used to, but I'm hoping that one day I'll be one of those people who get out and run five miles every day and say"—she punches the air and smiles mock-enthusiastically—"'I haven't missed a day in ten years.'"

Stephanie Duncan, Jen's trainer, strides up, and the two head off to a smaller private gym for her workout.

Duncan knows not to take it easy. Jen lifts hand weights and swings kettlebells, does lunges on a slideboard, jumps rope—enough to get any fit person's heart pumping. Jen is working hard, sweating, and complaining good-naturedly when told to do another rep. This workout isn't for wimps, but it is safe.

"Jen knows to tell me if she has any chest discomfort," Duncan says. "I don't ask her. I wait for her to tell me. I'm an exercise physiologist. This is a medical fitness center, so a lot of the cases we get here are medical issues. I would have to say that Jen is one of my fun clients because I can really push her. She is very strong."

Jen smiles proudly at this assessment and wipes the sweat from her brow. She knows her latest incident pulled her under for a time, but these days, things are looking up again. She's feeling stronger, both mentally and physically, and that's important. She's got kids to raise, a husband to love, and, in her role as Heart Association spokesperson, speeches to give.

She's also trying to shift her inner focus from the future to the present moment, because no one knows what will happen next. (That reality became all too clear to me as I scurried out of my doctor's office.) From here on out, Jen says, she is going to keep living her life out loud. For Jen, that's survival.

"I decided I can't take this part of my identity and hide it away," she says. "I'm unable to do that. So I'm going to go to the other extreme. I'll use my blog and my activism to share my story with anyone who wants to hear it. I'm going to continue to be myself and just bring heart-attack Jen along."

Chapter 2

How to Survive the Death of a Spouse

I was only eight at the time, but I still remember Norma's call. My mom answered the phone in her bedroom, listened quietly for a few moments, and then shut the door. After what felt like a long time, she emerged, her usually smiling mouth set in a tight, serious line.

"That was Norma," Mom said, letting out a deep breath. "Wally died." My mother, who'd lived through a war and rarely cried, looked shaken. Wally was her best friend's husband, a kind man I hardly knew, a decorated World War II veteran who'd lost his leg to a land mine. While I didn't know Wally very well, I did know Norma. She was the next-door neighbor with an infectious laugh, the first person my mother told when she suspected that, rather than going into early menopause at age forty-one, she was actually pregnant *again*, eleven years after giving birth to her fifth child.

I was that unexpected sixth pregnancy, and as the only kid still at home, I spent a lot of time with Norma and my mom, enjoying their jokes and easy camaraderie. But this situation was different. Something serious and scary had happened. As I scanned my mother's face for cues, the sadness slowly gave way to determination. She had a job to do.

"This is how deep our friendship was," recalls Norma, her memory still keen at age ninety-two. "I called your mother and told her that Wally had died. I said, 'I don't want to have a meal after the funeral at the church. I want it at my house. Would you take charge?' Your mom said she would and she organized that meal. I'm not sure how she did it: There were 135 people in my house that day and everybody got fed."

Worrying about feeding funeral guests seems like the last thing a person would think about just hours after losing her spouse of twenty-eight years. But from Norma's perspective, that's just the way things get done. She'd grown up in a small town during the Great Depression, and when people died there, she explained, the ones left behind turned to practical responsibilities, doing their grieving while cooking meals, sweeping the floors, and opening the windows to let in the fresh air.

When I was in my first year of college, I learned this Emily Dickinson poem:

The Bustle in a House
The Morning after Death
Is solemnest of industries
Enacted upon Earth —

The Sweeping up the Heart
And putting Love away
We shall not want to use again
Until Eternity —

My professor explained that the poem was a metaphor about the practical side of death, about the way people in Dickinson's day almost immediately turned to the real-life work of preparing a home for a wake or a funeral almost as a way to process their loss. This is what Norma did, and what my mom did.

By keeping their hands busy, they stayed in the land of the living, Norma says. "Wally had died, and I was very, very sad, but I knew that I couldn't give up. I had to keep on living."

From death, a new life

It's not that Wally's death wasn't a shock and a tragedy. The happily married couple had five children, two still teenagers. "Our relationship was very strong," Norma says. "We loved each other."

When Wally died, he and Norma were away from home at his

mother's eighty-fifth birthday party. A few years earlier, Wally had had a heart attack, but this was mid-1970s, years before angioplasty became a common treatment for patients with coronary artery disease. After his first attack, Wally received the standard treatment at the time: A weeklong hospital stay, and a bottle of nitroglycerine pills.

Norma recalls that on the night of his death, Wally seemed more tired than usual. "He usually stayed up later than I did," she says, "but that night he went upstairs to bed and his brother and I stayed up to watch the news."

When Norma finally came up to the bedroom, Wally had left the light on, so she read for a few minutes before falling asleep. "I was just drifting off," Norma says, "when there was this terrible commotion in the bed. I turned the light on and Wally pointed to his nitroglycerine. I put one under his tongue. By this time I was up and on his side of the bed. The next thing I knew he collapsed in my arms. I know now that by then he was already dead. I had just learned CPR, so I started it on him, but nothing worked. He never responded. The family called the local firemen to come, and they rushed Wally to the hospital. He was dead then. He was done, but nobody admitted that at the time. Even when we got to the hospital, the doctor kept pretending to do CPR on him. They were trying to protect me from the truth."

Norma felt blindsided by her husband's death. Her children did, too.

"The first heart attack was a warning, I know, but you're never really ready for it," she says. "If I'd spent my time thinking about the possibility of him having another heart attack after the first one, I'd never have been able to live a normal life. And I was living a normal life. We were very happy. I'd started a job that I loved, but I was still in the thick of raising our two youngest kids. I never thought I'd be a single mother. The kids never thought their dad could die." When Norma called home to tell her youngest children that their father had died, her daughter refused to talk to her on the phone, Norma remembers. "She said, 'No. That's not true. You are not my mother. You are somebody playing a Halloween joke.'"

But it wasn't a joke. It was the truth, and despite her no-nonsense approach to handling the practical details of her husband's death, Norma grieved. She cried, she got angry, she asked for—and accepted—help from friends. It took years for Norma to feel like she had healed from the experience, but she believes that the clear-eyed way she faced the reality of Wally's death made her recovery possible.

"I was a mess, but I went back to work about a week after Wally died," Norma says. (A couple of years earlier, she'd taken a full-time job as a volunteer coordinator at a nursing home.) "I couldn't stand to be at home," she says. "I had to go to work. The kids were in school and what would I do with myself alone all day? When I got to work there were tears, but there were also open arms. I loved being there. I loved those people. I didn't stay home any longer than I had to. The next Monday I went back to work. It's how I survived."

Another way that Norma made sense of her loss was symbolic.

"I was so sad, but I told myself, 'You are going to have another life. You have to accept it. Everything is different. Your whole life is changed,'" she says. "So I got a new pair of glasses. I went to the beauty shop and had my hair restyled. I bought a bunch of new clothes. I took lessons in tennis and golf and belly dancing. I realized that with Wally's death my life had changed forever. As deeply sad as that made me feel, there was nothing I could do about it. I told myself, 'Let's make this change positive.'"

This is a healthy response to the loss of a spouse, says Ellen Kamp, president and co-founder of W Connection, a New York–based support organization for widows. Not every widow feels comfortable making major life changes immediately following a death. But time does not stand still.

"The initial part of the bereavement journey is the realization that you are going to have to rebuild your life," Kamp says. "For many women, that change is very hard to accept, but I think it ends up being about choice. You have the choice to continue to live your life. No matter how much you may want to, you can't go back to your old life. The present doesn't stay still and wait for you. It's painful, but you have to keep living."

Kamp and W Connection co-founder Dawn Nargi became friends after Nargi's husband died of cancer at age forty-three and

Kamp, whose husband had died of a heart attack a year earlier, reached out to offer support and advice. The two quickly discovered that the friendship and support they provided each other was invaluable. "Only another widow can truly understand what a woman experiences when she loses her spouse," Kamp says. Resources for widows were few, they found, and none provided the support and understanding of another woman who'd been through a similar trauma. Building on the strength of their unique bond, Kamp and Nargi formed W Connection.

The organization is based around a comprehensive website that provides information about bereavement and links to resources for widows, plus a national peer-to-peer support program where widows offer guidance to other women who've lost a spouse.

"We found that the people who helped us the most were not therapists or traditional support groups, but other women like us, women who'd lost their spouses," says Kamp, who left her high-powered job in New York's financial-services industry to lead W Connection. "Both Dawn and I felt that while the deaths of our husbands were extraordinary tragedies, we thought that something bigger needed to come out of our losses. We wanted to help others, and this is the best way we know how."

The Casserole Brigade

Before she died, Sam Feldman's wife gave him a warning.

"She knew that men who live longer than their wives are in the minority," Feldman recalls with a quiet chuckle. "Because of that fact, she knew I'd be an especially desirable commodity once she was gone. So she laid a caveat on me: She said that after she was gone, I couldn't accept casseroles with e-mail addresses attached to them. The ratio of widows to widowers is seven or eight to one, and she wanted me to avoid the 'Casserole Brigade.'"

At the time, Feldman wasn't thinking about such things. Gretchen, his beloved wife of fifty-three years, was dying of lung cancer. The two had met back in 1955 on a blind date arranged by a neighbor. They hit it off almost immediately, and married a year and a half later. At the time of Gretchen's death, they had two grown daughters and split their time between their home on Martha's Vineyard and their apartment in New York City.

Gretchen, who'd graduated from Swarthmore with a degree in art history, worked in a museum as a textile conservator. Feldman ran his family's retail business.

"We had a great relationship," Feldman says. "I was the pragmatist, the business person and the money person. She was able to indulge her interest in art and raising a family."

Gretchen was in good health, so the couple was surprised to learn in November 2007, after a mammogram and a subsequent screening X-ray at the hospital on Martha's Vineyard, that she had stage IV lung cancer that had spread to her liver.

"She was completely asymptomatic," Feldman says. "We walked for an hour every day. We worked out. We were shocked and devastated."

The next day they went into the city, to meet with doctors at Sloan-Kettering Cancer Center. Doctors put Gretchen on a chemotherapy regimen, which worked well for seven months. "But then she got sicker and sicker," Feldman says. "She died in our New York apartment. We had hospice for a week at home. She died exactly a year after the diagnosis on November 9, 2008. It was an awful year."

During the year of Gretchen's illness, Feldman committed himself to her care. He took her to doctor appointments, talked to friends, and administered medications. Though he knew intellectually that Gretchen was dying, he never really accepted it until the moment she died.

"Her death was devastating to me, even though I should've been prepared for it," he says. "I think it's something you can't prepare for, an experience that is very difficult to share with anyone else. You can't understand it unless you've been there."

Feldman, a usually optimistic, take-charge person, took his wife's death hard. "It was total devastation to me," he says. "I was a basket case. I think I would've done myself in, but I had trouble. I was thinking of putting my car in the garage and turning on the engine, but I realized I couldn't do it because it was a Prius with no

emissions." He pauses for effect, before adding, "That's a joke."
(Ba-dum-bum.)

For a time, Feldman tells me that he had a hard time getting
out of the house, but he knew he had to connect with others or he'd
never recover. Though he grieved for his wife every minute of every
day, he didn't really want to die himself. All he needed was a reason
to get up in the morning. So he called the local hospice, and asked
about bereavement groups. He found out that such a group existed—
but only women attended.

Feldman asked if the hospice could provide names of men
whose wives had recently died. He contacted a handful and asked
them out to lunch. It turned out to be a cathartic event for all the men
who attended.

"We told our stories and we cried together," Feldman says. "I
said, 'Why don't we start getting together on a regular basis to talk
about how we feel about getting on in life after the loss of our wives?'
The bond of grief was such a common denominator that turned
this group into friends that could talk in the meetings. As each new
member came in, they felt like they could express their emotions in a
way they couldn't comfortably in a mixed-gender group."

Because Feldman is an entrepreneur and a jump-starter, a person who doesn't enjoy sitting still, he explained to me that he decided
to build on the success of his men's grief group. Perhaps because
fewer men outlive their wives, they often struggle to find organized
support networks, so he poured his enthusiasm into the creation
of the National Widowers' Organization. As Feldman conceived it,
the National Widowers' Organization provides online advice and
support for widowers, plus assistance establishing local widowers'
groups. The organization also runs a national network of one-on-
one peer phone counselors.

The group, which operates with the help of Executive Director
Fred Spero, has been a lifeline for Feldman, a way for him to think that
he is making something good out of the trauma of his wife's death.

"I'm a start-up guy," Feldman says. "Starting the National Widowers' Organization was instinctive. I had a basic need or desire to
help other people. It might have even been a selfish motivation in my

need for healing, but I was able to help other people and help myself at the same time."

The group is trying to fill the gap between a loved one's death and the next stage in a person's life.

"In some ways, the loss of a spouse is a predicable event," Spero says. "It is going to happen to everyone. What is not done in our society is planning for the emotional aspect, for how do you transition from a death. We also don't acknowledge the impact a spouse's death has on the rest of the family or on society. People tend to think that grief will just pass in time, but it won't unless those left behind get the support they need. This is what our organization is trying to do."

The speed of light

Almost from the moment of her first date with John, it was like Stacey's life shifted into fast-forward. The pair, young professionals living in Boston, were matched up by mutual friends. They'd met each other in passing before, but it wasn't until John and Stacey finally spent time alone together that their strong attraction became obvious. They had so much in common. They enjoyed each other's company. They were fully grown adults. They didn't see any reason to take it slow.

Stacey laughs as she tells me, openly, "We had a fast courtship. We actually slept together on our first date. That was in April 2003. We moved in together in July of that year and married in August of '04. So it was just 16 months between when we went on that date and when we got married."

It wasn't like Stacey was known for her impulsiveness. She'd always been hard working and studious. After a post-college stint in the Peace Corps, she and a friend moved to Boston to look for jobs. Stacey got a job as an editor at a small publishing company. A native Oregonian, she missed the West Coast, but was building a good life in the East when she met John. Jumping into a life together felt natural, easy.

"It was one of those decisions that wasn't a decision," Stacey says. "It was just understood that we would live our lives together. It was kind of a mind meld. We were on the same page about so many big life issues."

In the months leading up to their wedding, John's stomach started to hurt. John thought the pains were a symptom of stress: His job as a teacher was hard—and then there was the wedding planning. "In most ways, he seemed absolutely fine," Stacey says. "Any symptoms or general *malaise* he was feeling we would always write off to his job. But the symptoms did intensify. We both thought, 'Maybe it's gallstones.' He went to his general practitioner."

John's doctor ran blood tests, which reported elevated liver function. The day before the wedding, the doctor called to tell John he didn't have hepatitis, which was a relief. Before hanging up, the doctor told John to enjoy his wedding and come back for more tests after the honeymoon. Elevated liver function is a common indicator of cancer, but Stacey and John didn't focus on that possibility. The doctor had told them to enjoy their wedding and honeymoon, and they did.

Stacey tells me she's grateful that the doctor gave them time to enjoy their wedding free from the cloud of cancer.

"I am almost positive that the doctor strongly suspected that John had cancer at that moment," she says. "But this little gift of time allowed us to go forward with our wedding and have a really wonderful time. We were somewhat concerned, but the worst we thought it could be once we realized it wasn't hepatitis was it must be something wacky and random."

After the wedding, John went back for more tests. Three weeks later, doctors discovered cancerous tumors. He was diagnosed with pancreatic cancer.

"Getting John's diagnosis and learning about how serious it was was the hardest thing I've gone through to date including him dying," Stacey says, softly. "I don't have words to describe how empty and bereft and cheated and angry I felt. It was like going through the five stages of grief repeatedly for weeks on end. It was horrible."

Though they felt crippled by grief and shock, the couple, both rational, science-respecting types, eventually regrouped, got online, and researched pancreatic cancer. The news wasn't good.

"From what we learned on the Internet, we were looking at him living for a matter of months," Stacey says. In the end, John beat the odds, living for two and a half years after his diagnosis. He kept working full time until the last four months of his life. Most of that time, Stacey told me, he felt well.

"It was surprising to me how quickly your physical and mental lives adapt to a new sense of normal," she says. "John's chemo date was Wednesday. He'd pick me up and we'd go out to lunch. It was a little date. For us the decision was, 'Let's have our life remain as normal as possible.' We had to make certain adjustments in our lives because John was often very tired. But for the time that we had we wanted to have as normal a life as possible. We went on vacations. We visited our families. We just kept living."

John's parents—traditionally minded Korean immigrants— pressured the couple to focus their attention completely on fighting John's cancer. But John and Stacey resisted letting it take over their lives. They felt confident in John's medical team, and they were committed to following through with their treatment recommendations. John even tried a few alternative therapies, but saw limited success. In the end, the focus was on living a normal life.

"We just both felt like it would be ridiculously depressing to have John's cancer be the focus of our lives," Stacey says. "We needed to enjoy some time together. Doing research about other doctors and about pancreatic cancer was not the way we wanted to spend our time. I don't blame John's parents for feeling that way. If it were my child, I might feel the same way. But we just couldn't live like that."

For Stacey and John, part of living a normal life included having children. Because John's chemotherapy could affect his fertility, he banked sperm, and once his treatment regime was set and the couple had settled into a gradual acceptance of their shifted lives, Stacey underwent in vitro fertilization (IVF). She became pregnant with twins on the first attempt.

Even though Stacey knew she would have to raise their children alone, she still was overjoyed about the pregnancy. "John had always wanted to be a father," she says. "And I loved him and wanted to have children with him. We figured that once his treatment plan was on track and we started to see some improvement in his numbers, we would do the kid thing right away." If she had any fears about what might happen in the future, Stacey put them aside. "While the thought of being a single mom was terrifying to me, I thought there were plenty of people who had done it and made it," she says. "I didn't want to be ruled by my own fears in the face of something I knew was really important to both of us."

Stacey's pregnancy progressed normally, and during that time John responded well to his treatment. When their twins—a boy and a girl—were born in 2006, he was feeling healthy. Because he was a teacher, John had seven weeks off in the summer after his children's birth: He was proud to be able to fully participate in the twins' early life.

"That was the time in his illness that he felt the best he ever felt," Stacey says. "He did surprisingly well during that time. He'd get up in the night to help with feedings."

By Christmastime, John's health started to decline. Just as the babies were learning to sleep through the night, Stacey told me, her husband started to feel terrible.

From the moment John got his cancer diagnosis, Stacey tried to stay optimistic. Though she knew that the odds were not in their favor, she also had a nagging feeling that if she gave up hope that his treatments would keep the disease at bay, she might not be able to survive. For more than two years, she kept up hope. Then, without warning, she tells me now, "around the first of the year, the beginning of 2007, it became clear that John . . . ," Stacey's voice over the phone falters for a moment before she takes a deep breath and continues, "It was then that we both knew that he wasn't going to feel better this time, that the cancer was finally winning. That was really scary. That was when I had that realization that this is it. I now needed to figure out how I could do this by myself."

Together John and Stacey talked about how she could handle the practical side of parenting twins alone. John encouraged her to start by trying out basic things like giving two squirming babies a bath. "At that point, he was still there and still able to help," she says. "Later, when he wasn't feeling well, I'd do stuff by myself, and because I'd practiced doing it beforehand, I was more confident when the time finally came."

By the early spring 2007, John's condition worsened significantly. In late March the oncologist suggested they seek hospice care, and by early April it became clear that he wouldn't live much longer. Stacey told me that for some time, she'd accepted that this would eventually happen, but every day up to the end she hoped that she'd have more time with her husband. Though it felt like a lifetime, she actually hadn't known John for all that long. They'd only been together for a few years, and now their life together was about to end.

"I had already accepted that this was going to happen," Stacey says, trying to explain for me the way her mind began to shift with John's worsening health. "All along, I knew that his death was inevitable, but that didn't mean that I was at peace with it." Then, when the end was near, the thought of John's death "didn't have that same sharp, painful-edge feeling that it had when we first heard that his cancer was terminal." She continues, "Instead, it was this leaden, horrible feeling: sad, but not panicky. That was what I was left with."

John died in their Boston apartment on April 12, 2007.

Is anybody out there?

When she learned that her husband had incurable pancreatic cancer, Stacey felt alone. Mostly she felt alone because she was afraid of what her life might be like after her husband died. But she also felt alone because her situation was so unusual. Pancreatic cancer is usually an older person's disease: The average age at diagnosis is seventy-two. But John was just thirty-two when he found out that he had the disease. Support groups and other resources were designed for people in a different stage of life, Stacey says.

"I did one therapy group, a telephone support group for caregivers of people who had pancreatic cancer," Stacey says. "That group was somewhat helpful to me, but I was the only one in my age group. From the emotional side, we were all dealing with the potential loss of a significant person in our lives, but the actual life circumstances were so different. I didn't fit in."

Still, Stacey, an extrovert, needed to communicate with other people about what was going on in her life. In the fall of 2005, a little more than a year after John's diagnosis and just as she was starting the process of IVF, Stacey got on her computer and began to blog. She knew that everything she posted online could be visible to the world, but at first she considered her writing to be private, a sort of electronic journal. Nobody would find it, she reasoned. She didn't even tell John what she was doing.

Then someone commented on her first post. This public exposure of her feelings felt unnerving at first, but also strangely comforting. Curious, Stacey cautiously made her first ventures into the blogosphere and, surprisingly, found other people who were experiencing similar situations.

"I found other blogs like mine," blogs about young women whose spouses had cancer, she says. "I began commenting and leaving my URL with my comments. Then I started to get more readers. It snowballed." The blog quickly became a support group, a place where Stacey could share her grief and frustration with people who understood what she was going through.

"Other young cancer widows are out there online and we found each other through this blog," Stacey says. "We comment on each other's blogs, we support each other through hard times like anniversaries of spouses' deaths. I've made real-life connections."

The Web has been a great source of connection and solace for many widows and widowers, says W Connection's Ellen Kamp. "The experience of being a widow—especially being a young widow—can feel extremely isolating. While in-person interactions are an important part of the healing process, just being able to go online and easily find others who've been where you are is a revelation. It's an amazing recovery tool."

Years after John's death, years after she left Boston with her children to live closer to family in her native Portland, Stacey's readers continue to follow her and comment on her posts.

"At first I thought I'd never find anybody who understood what I was going through," Stacey says, "but through blogging, I found my people, virtual strangers who helped me through many tough times. It's the real power of the Internet."

These days, Stacey continues to chronicle her life online, writing about her struggles to parent alone and her memories of John, but her posts have dwindled in number as her focus shifts from the past to the present—and even the future. Sometimes Stacey feels guilty for being neglectful of her blog, but then she reminds herself that the inactivity is a good thing. It means that she's still alive and growing, no longer living in the past.

One more step

Some people have months, maybe even years, to prepare for the death of a loved one. But Mary never even got the chance to say goodbye.

On Thanksgiving weekend 2003, Mary, her husband, Wim, and their six-year-old son were driving home to Chicago from a friend's house in Spring Green, Wisconsin.

"My husband had a cold," Mary tells me. "He maybe wasn't feeling 100 percent well. He was driving. We were at a four-way stop. He thought the other party was going to stop and he drove right into their path. The people who hit us were driving a small truck with a horse trailer. They called 911. My last memory of the accident is of my husband saying, 'Oh my god. He's not going to stop.' I have lost all memory from that second until I was in the ambulance on my way to the hospital. My son and I were taken to Beloit. My husband was taken to Rockford. He died there. I never saw him again."

Mary was a private-school librarian in Chicago and her husband was a university mathematics professor. They were older parents: Mary gave birth to her only son when she was in her mid-forties. The trio was a small, self-contained family. Wim was Dutch and all of his relatives lived in Holland. Mary, a South African, had just one nephew who lived in the United States. After the accident, a friend drove to Beloit to pick Mary and her son up from the hospital and Wim's brothers flew from the Netherlands to help with the funeral.

Like the hours after the accident, Mary hardly remembers

anything from the days that followed. She was in shock, she says now. Her life was a painful blur, something she really doesn't want to revisit.

"I suppose it is probably my brain's way of protecting me from the reality," Mary says about her blackout. (She tells me that she's been told she could probably recover memories through hypnosis, but she says that for now she'd prefer to keep them locked away in her subconscious.) Though she felt deep despair and crushing sadness in the wake of the accident, Mary also knew deep down that she had to keep living. She had a young son who needed her; She put her head down and soldiered on. Living this way, Mary realizes now, was the only way she could cope with the daunting reality of her life. Her journey to healing was going to be long and she needed to conserve her energy.

"About six months after the accident I realized that I was existing in a tunnel," Mary says. "It was how I survived everything that was being thrown at me, scary, frustrating things like insurance claims. For a long time I didn't open the letters. I ignored them and just kept them in a box. I knew I had to get through the tunnel in order to keep life going. But I only allowed in as much as I could cope with. When there were things that I just didn't want to deal with, I set them aside for later."

Looking back on those days, Mary now believes that her singular focus was key to her survival.

"I used to hike," she says. "When I was really exhausted on a long hike, I'd count my steps just to get to the next step." *Just one more step.* "For a long time after my husband died, my life felt very much like that. Every day was just another step."

For Mary, living step by step meant that the less essential things needed to get set aside. It was like weeding a garden: The weeds that were choking out the essentials got pulled and tossed out.

"At some level I decided as long as I wasn't starving and I had enough money, I could let the other things go," she says.

One thing she couldn't let go was the care of her son. At first she congratulated herself for being able to get him dressed and fed and put in bed every day. But he needed more—and he let her know.

"My husband always got up in the morning with our son," Mary says, "and he was the one who gave our son his breakfast. He'd read to him while he was eating. In the beginning, I couldn't imagine finding time for that. I was just focused on frantically getting out the door."

But her son made it clear that morning time with a parent was essential.

"He was missing that warmth and attention in the morning," Mary says. "At that time, right after his father's death, the last thing I *was* was warm. My son wanted to be read to: He was six years old. We devised a compromise where he would help me with breakfast—and I would have time to sit with him while he ate."

For the first few years after Wim's death, Mary avoided seeing a therapist because she felt like she didn't want to rip the bandage off her emotional wounds. Her son had his own therapist. Mary went along for several sessions in the beginning, but she stopped going after a few months. She tells me that she felt she needed to focus on the day-to-day, like going to work and raising her son. She didn't want to focus on her own emotional state.

"For several years, I needed to put my head down and focus," she says. "That other stuff felt like a distraction."

In recent years, the pain has dulled. Mary's son is older now and more independent, and she has decided that she's ready to spend more time working through her own emotions. She's seeing a therapist to work through her feelings.

"One of the things that my counselor had me do was to write a letter to my husband thanking him for leaving," Mary tells me, slowly. At first it seemed impossible that Mary could ever find something to be thankful for about that horrible, unfair accident. But with time and painful discussion, she was able to isolate several good things that have grown out of the bad. "Because my husband died, I have a different relationship with my son," Mary says. "We are probably much closer than we would have been if his father had lived. He looks after me. I'm very protective of him."

Leave taking

For three years, Mary and her son stayed in the house they'd lived in with Wim. To Mary, it felt important not to make too many changes too quickly, but the house was a 45-minute drive to her work and her son's school. "I felt uncomfortable spending too much time in the car," she says. "It didn't feel safe, and the house felt too big and too expensive for the two of us." At first, Mary's son resisted the move; he didn't want to leave his father behind. But then her counselor helped talk them both through the move, and by the time they left their suburban home for a new place in the city, Mary's son was actually more ready to go than she was.

On moving day, the therapist "came over and we conducted a ceremony," Mary says, "to make sure that my husband's spirit would come with us to our new home and not be left behind. My son was nine at the time, and I think it helped him feel better about the move. It helped me, too." The ceremony was a way for Mary and her son to say goodbye to one place, a place filled with happy—and horrible—memories, and move on to the next part of their lives. Unlike the sudden, jarring shock of Wim's death, they got to make this move on their own schedule.

During one of our conversations, Mary tells me that she sees herself as a logical person, not the slightest bit superstitious or New Age-y. But the leave-taking ceremony, complete with its significant words and the smell of burning sage, was just what she needed. It wasn't a funeral: That had already happened three years before. But it was a ritual of her own design, an opportunity to celebrate Wim's life at a less painful moment.

"Maybe it was a little flaky," Mary says with a cynical snort, "but we said goodbye, and that was important." While Mary knew that she and her son would always carry Wim's memory in their hearts, she also knew that with this move they were taking an important step toward making space in their hearts for other things. It was just one step toward healing, but it was an important one.

In a joyful place

For the first seven years after Wim's death, Mary couldn't think about dating. But two years ago, not long after she and her son had moved to their new home, she took the first tentative steps, signing up for a dating site.

At first, "Nobody contacted me," she says. She blames her age. "That was rough because I felt like I had jumped off a cliff when I put my profile together and then nobody responded. I felt vulnerable. It made me realize I have lost a lot of confidence in myself in the last nine years. My husband was the gregarious one in our relationship. I don't like going to parties by myself. I find it scary to go out and meet people." Discouraged, Mary stepped away for a time, but now, at age sixty, she's decided to try again. So far she's had informal coffee dates with a few men. She's not sure she's looking for love, she told me: She'd probably settle for companionship. "I've heard that sixty-year-old men only want to date forty-five-year-old women," she laughs. "I'm not interested in a seventy-year-old man, so I'm hoping that I'll find someone who's more realistic."

Mary is not going to pin her future happiness on the dating scene. One thing she's learned from Wim's death is that no matter what horrible blows you've been dealt, your happiness lies in your own hands.

"I think we bring to the world what we make of it," Mary says. "That's something I try to pass on to my son. Sure, I'm fairly cynical about the world. I know that things don't always go the way we've planned, but I do think that your happiness is dependent on your own actions. I'm going to choose to be happy and make life decisions that will move me in that direction. Some people are born miserable and make themselves miserable all the time. That is not my nature. My nature is to try to make the best of where I am."

And where Mary is, increasingly, is a joyful place.

"A year ago I felt a lightness that I hadn't felt before," she says. "I was walking to school with my son in the spring. I had this 'it's a beautiful day' feeling. It was wonderful. A basic sense of joy was gone from my life for two years. Joy is the only word I can think of. It's still not something that is always present, but it is something that starts to feel possible again."

Survival tips for widows and widowers from people who've been there:

+ **Remember you are still among the living,** Norma says. But don't be afraid to grieve. While she let herself cry and question and lean on friends for help, Norma found great strength in "just pulling myself together and going on living my life," she says. "I felt like going back to work and putting one foot in front of the other was the best therapy I could have. Keeping living my life after my husband died kept me sane."

+ **Reach out to others in similar situations,** advise Ellen Kamp and Dawn Negri, founders of W Connection. "When a spouse dies, a person can feel horribly and totally alone," Kamp says. "For me, talking to other widows helped pull me out of the hole I'd dug for myself after my husband passed. I could learn from them, and, as time went on, other, newer widows could learn from me."

+ Sam Feldman, founder of the National Widowers' Organization, believes that **different genders grieve differently.** Sometimes it helps to seek out single-gender support groups. "I don't have anything against women or widows," he laughs, "but I do think that the best way for a man to overcome the death of his wife is to be with other men. We have different ways of offering advice, counsel and support."

+ **Search for support and connections in nontraditional formats,** says Stacey. After her husband died of pancreatic cancer in his mid-thirties, she built her strongest support network online. "Because the disease usually strikes people when they are older, the official support groups are usually designed for older people," she says. Through blogging and other online networking, Stacey was able to build a network of other young widows. "For me, it really was a lifesaver."

+ Surviving a loved one's death takes time, Mary believes. **Be patient with yourself, and focus only on the bare essentials—if that's all you feel you can handle.** "There is no official timeline for grief," she says. "And the pain is different for everyone. Once I accepted that fact, I was able to slowly start building my own recovery. It didn't matter what other people thought I should be doing."

Chapter 3
How to Survive Chronic Illness

A small, smiling, birdlike woman, Dee moves gingerly as she rises from her easy chair to greet me. She's wearing a large neck brace and has one arm in a sling, but she's smiling, a smile that takes up the lower half of her face and makes the skin around her kind eyes crinkle. The month before, Dee was in a car accident, and because her bones are weakened by osteoporosis, she broke her neck, back, rib and sternum. No one else in the car was seriously injured.

Dee, you see, has many health problems, and, in the awkward juggle unique to modern medicine, she takes many drugs to treat those problems—and still many others to treat the life-threatening side effects of the drugs prescribed to save her life. Dee, sixty-nine, keeps her drugs in a tackle box. It's easier to haul them around that way, she says, and the tackle box is smaller than the "washtub" in which many of the drugs were first presented to her twenty-two years ago after she survived a then-groundbreaking kidney-pancreas transplant surgery. (Dee's osteoporosis, for example, is a side effect of the steroid drugs she's taken since the operation to limit organ rejection.)

But Dee's health problems actually started much longer ago. In 1968, when she was pregnant with her first child, Dee became sick with what was first diagnosed as gestational diabetes. After her daughter, Kim, was born, Dee's diabetes did not go away as it usually does for women with the condition. Instead she became an insulin-dependent, or "brittle" diabetic, with difficult-to-control fluctuations in her insulin levels.

A trained nutritionist, Dee was religious about following a diabetic diet. She measured her blood glucose levels carefully, and

51

followed her doctors' orders to the letter. Still, for Dee, it was hard to keep the disease under control. She experienced wild fluctuations in her blood sugar and multiple diabetic reactions, including blackouts, erratic behavior, and memory loss.

After years of her struggling with the disease, diabetes injured parts of Dee's body. For a time, she became legally blind—though laser surgery restored vision to one of her eyes; painful neuropathy reduced sensation in her hands and feet and made walking difficult; and her kidneys eventually failed, forcing Dee to go on dialysis. In 1989, seriously ill and desperate for a respite from the life-diminishing stress of dialysis, Dee volunteered for the then-experimental double transplant. Against all odds—the donor match wasn't exact—Dee's transplant was a success. The donor organs made a home in her body and keep working steadily nearly twenty-five years later.

While the pancreas transplant cured Dee of her diabetes, it did not cure her of the physical limitations that existed before the surgery. She lives with a challenging combination of chronic diseases, but she is determined not to let illnesses define her life.

"You will never hear my mom complain," says Dee's daughter, Kim. This morning, she's the one who opens the front door of her parents' lovely suburban house, ushering me in, serving me lunch. Her mom is taking it slowly in the days after the accident, and Kim hovers around her protectively.

"Mom's had so many illnesses so much of her life, but she tries really hard not to make her life all about being sick," Kim says. "She could, but she doesn't. I don't know anybody else like that. Sometimes I think," here Kim pauses to smile, knowingly, "that her stubborn attitude is what keeps her moving forward despite all the stuff that threatens to hold her back."

Chronic illness is part of life for nearly half of all Americans. According to the U.S. Centers for Disease Control and Prevention, in 2005, 133 million U.S. citizens—almost one out of every two adults—had at least one chronic condition. The treatment and prevention of chronic illness is a serious public health issue: Seven out of ten deaths in the United States are a result of chronic disease.

Dee's case is more extreme than most—chronic illness, or a

disease lasting three months or more, is a loosely defined term, with many variations of severity and impact—but her perspective is helpful for anyone facing serious health challenges. Despite facing serious, even life-threatening disease, Dee has learned to live a happy, productive, loving life.

"I want people to realize that every morning when the sun comes out, you have been given a new day," Dee tells me. "It's a gift. Everything is starting over again. Forget about the last day. I think there are too many people who don't look toward the next day and think positive, uplifting thoughts. I survive by lifting my spirits up."

What it takes

While a positive, stubborn attitude is a major part of Dee's survival strategy, she also says that her physical survival is also ensured by the drugs that fill her tackle box. While she hates the hassle of taking handfuls of pills every day, Dee accepts the fact that these drugs are needed to keep her alive.

Off the top of her head, Dee recites a partial list of her medications. "I take prednisone, Plavix, a few anti-rejection drugs. I take a drug for heart attack and a baby aspirin. I take a statin because of my cholesterol. I also take two blood-pressure medicines. For myself to feel good, I take a 1,000 mg of vitamin C in the morning and again at night. That also helps with my immune system. Because of my medications, I'm more apt to catch infections. I also take a vitamin D to help with my absorption of my calcium supplement. And I take zinc to help with my immune system."

The pills go down in "a mouthful," Dee tells me. "In the morning I take fourteen, and then at night I only take four."

In an ideal world, Dee's life would be free of medicine and medical professionals, but ever since the day back in 1968 when the doctor first gave her the diagnosis of diabetes, she's known that will never be the case. Instead, Dee assembled a team of "helpers," people dedicated to keeping her as healthy and strong as possible. A committed, serious student, Dee follows medical professionals' instructions religiously, doing whatever it takes to maintain her health.

And though Dee usually tends to follow doctors' orders, she's always been her own best advocate, researching procedures, drugs, and side effects and raising concerns when she thinks treatments may negatively impact her quality of life.

That serious, focused nature was there from the start, says Jean, one of Dee's closest childhood friends. She tells me a favorite memory from their teen years growing up in rural Illinois. "We played in the band together. Dee played oboe and I played flute. During practice I would giggle and joke with my other friends, but while the other kids were distracted and goofing around, Dee would just keep playing, her little foot tapping in perfect rhythm. She was focused. She followed the director. That's the way she's lived her life, and for Dee's health, that turned out to be a very good attribute. She can figure out what's essential and she stays with it, with virtually no complaining."

Dee's team of helpers includes seven doctors. She says, "I have the transplant center. I've also had two heart attacks, so I have a cardiologist. I have problems with neuropathy, so I have a podiatrist. I have to have insoles and orthotics. Because of all the transplant drugs I take, I have a lot of skin cancer. So I have a skin-cancer oncologist. And then there's the osteoporosis. For a time, I was on Fosomax to help build up my calcium, but I've had bone issues in my jaw and problems with my teeth because of that. So I see a special dentist, too."

When Dee's diabetes was first diagnosed, she was the newest of new mothers. She learned to sterilize syringes and mix insulin while taking care of a tiny newborn, somehow managing to figure out how to measure her glucose levels and read her own body cues.

Dee fought hard to keep her family's lives as normal as possible. She didn't want her diabetes to impact them. Some people with diabetes make their families stick to the same diet—or limit their activities. Dee did her best not to do that. "I didn't want my health to affect my family and my husband and our lives together," she tells me, seriously. "I wanted them to live a normal life and I would work my way around that."

When Kim was older, Dee and her husband, Don, adopted their son, Jason. Here was another place to train her focus: Dee believes that her two children kept her going through hard times, times when her health faltered and her hope flagged. With kids to care for, she had to get out of bed in the morning, even if she didn't feel like it. "I didn't have time to sit around and feel sorry for myself," Dee says.

"As a kid," Kim recalls, "I really never felt cheated in any way because my mom always put me or my brother first."

Kim tells me that for the first years of her life, her mother's diabetes was fairly easy to ignore, but as the years went on, the disease did start to take a more obvious toll. At first Dee was able to control her blood sugars with just one shot of insulin a day, but by the time Kim was in high school and early college, Dee needed to give herself as many as eight shots a day. Her health became more precarious, and that reality wore on her family.

"I don't look back on my childhood and say, 'Oh wow. That was horrible,'" Kim tells me. "I remember most of the time my mom was pretty normal. Then into my high school years, it was starting to be more"—here Kim's eyes fill with tears—"more hard to ignore. She was really sick and there was no way to deny it. I would go to school and seem happy on the outside, but inside I felt like my world was falling apart."

When Jason was young, Dee's blood-sugar levels became particularly difficult to control. She did her best to anticipate when she would need to inject insulin, but there were times when the situation got the best of her. Once, when Jason was just four years old, Dee was driving him home from the grocery store when she went into insulin shock. She drove the car into oncoming traffic, and, according to family lore, the preschool-aged Jason leaned over (this was in the days before car seats) grabbed the wheel, steered the car into a ditch and turned the key off, shutting down the engine.

Excitedly, Dee's husband Don repeats the rest of the story. "The next vehicle to come along was an ambulance and they see this car sitting there with an adult and a four-year-old in it and they pick her up." Don pauses, his voice growing more serious. "Then the police got involved and that's the first I knew about this. They called me and said they are taking her to the hospital. They said, 'We think she's drunk.' I said, 'She's not drunk. Look in her wallet. She's diabetic.'"

There were other incidents like this, times when Dee's blood-sugar levels dropped so low that she slipped into a coma. More than once, she was discovered by a friend and rushed to the hospital. Other times, Dee slipped into shock while she was asleep in bed. Don woke in the middle of the night to feel the sheets wet with his wife's perspiration. Sometimes she'd let out a scream that would wake him up.

"You just get used to it," Don says about living with his wife's precarious health. He, along with their daughter, son, and close friends, takes a lead role in Dee's helper team. "I'm often thinking that I might lose her. I don't live my life like I am going to walk into the closet and find her dead there. But someday it could happen."

Love from above

It would be irresponsible to talk bout Dee's survival without talking about her faith. A committed Christian since childhood, Dee gives God credit for nearly everything that has happened in her life. Dee's faith is a living, strong faith. She prays every day, all the time. Sometimes her prayers are of petition, asking God for help or guidance, but mostly Dee says that her prayers are of thanks.

"A lot of time what I am praying is, 'Thank you, Lord,'" she tells me. Since 1989, the success of her transplanted organs has been a great source of prayer. "In the decades since I've had my transplant, I say this same prayer every single day and every night. I say, 'Lord, thank you for my pancreas, my eyesight, my feet that I can walk with, and my hands that I can hold things with.'"

For Dee, prayer is a regular part of life, not something she sets special time aside for. She'll pray in bed, while walking, before eating, even in the shower. She learned this approach from her mom, a strong woman who survived a childhood bout with polio and grew up to survive a life of hard work on the family farm.

"My mother said to me, 'If I had to set aside time to be on my knees and pray, I wouldn't get it done. So I pray while I'm working,'" Dee says. She takes the same approach as her mother, weaving prayer into everything she does. That running dialogue with God has infused Dee with a faith that no matter what challenges are dished out in life, she will always be cared for.

"I remember when I was seven or eight years old," Dee says, "I was afraid of the dark. My mother woke me up and she said, 'I want to take you on a little walk. I want to show you that God is with you all the time: day, night, when you are happy, when you are sad.' We walked about a quarter mile in the pitch dark down this dirt road and I wasn't afraid. From then on I didn't care about anything. I never worried. I'd leave the house open, unlocked." This sense of ease is also tied to Dee's belief in an afterlife. "I just trusted that if something bad is going to happen, it's going to happen, but in the end I will be fine."

Sometimes, that blind trust in the universe fills Dee with peace and happiness. "There are times when I just sing in the house by myself," she tells me. "It helps me feel better, and that way I don't remember the bad things. I sing to myself in the house because I feel so joyful inside."

In the middle of this conversation, Don breaks in. He gestures toward his wife, his normally guarded eyes open and earnest. It's clear that it's important that I hear what he has to say. "I don't know if you've ever interviewed anyone like her, but the first time I laid eyes on this lady she had a halo around her head," he says, slowly. "It was an aura, a glow. And I'm not kidding you. It was there." Then Don starts to sound a little sheepish, and a tone of teasing sneaks into his voice. "I guess I don't know if it was something to do with the lighting," he says. Then he switches gears again. "I don't know. But it was there."

Still, after all these years, Don thinks Dee's aura is there most of the time, even on days when her halo slips. While his religious faith hasn't always been as strong as his wife's, he does see her prayer, hopefulness, and positivity as somehow intertwined.

Still human

It's important to talk about the times Dee's halo slips. Though much of what I've written about her so far makes it seem like she's an infallible saint, Dee's not perfect, and she wouldn't want anyone to think that she was.

Like everyone, Dee's had her moments, days—and even weeks— when her relentlessly positive attitude doesn't feel like enough. One of those times was when Dee's kidneys failed and she had to go to dialysis three days a week. Back then, Don was working full time as a pilot for a major airline (he's since retired). Work took him away from home much of the week, Kim was away at college, and Jason was in school all day. Dee's eyes were weak back then, and Jean volunteered to drive her friend to treatments on days Don couldn't be there.

While dialysis was a lifesaver for Dee, it also was a serious trial. She had to limit her fluid intake to just two cups a day. Her diet was even more restricted than usual, with an emphasis on foods high in protein and limits on anything containing phosphorous, sodium, or potassium. Each dialysis session lasted three to four hours and left Dee feeling tired and washed out. This new routine took a toll. Dee's weight plummeted to 91 pounds. ("I'm usually closer to 110," the petite Dee tells me.) She was tired all the time and felt depressed. It hurt to walk, hurt to think, hurt to do much other than sleep.

One day, Dee decided she just wasn't going to get out of bed. She was tired of going to dialysis, and no one was going to make her. She didn't care what happened. When Jean arrived to drive her to her appointment, Dee wasn't dressed and waiting for her like she usually was.

"I went into the house," Jean says, "and Dee was still in bed. She was not going to go. She said, 'I am not doing this anymore.' I had to fight her to get her out of bed. I finally hauled her out. I helped her take her clothes off. I said, 'You are going to get in that shower. You have to do this to survive.' I got her dressed. Her hair was matted to her head. This was not like her."

When they finally arrived at the dialysis center, Jean requested a wheelchair for her friend. It was the only way they were going to get Dee into the building. It was strange and upsetting to see her friend, this positive, cheery woman she calls the "greatest little angel shepherd from heaven," so morose and hopeless. But it also made Jean feel good to be able to help.

"Dee was just tired that day" is how Jean says it now. "It's very difficult to have to get hooked up and sit there three times a week. It's really tough to stick with the diet and all the restrictions. Dee had a child at home, and the dialysis took a lot out of her. She wanted a better quality of life, and at that point, she couldn't see how she was ever going to get that."

The only way for Dee to regain her quality of life was for her to undergo a transplant. At that point in history, kidney transplants were common, but transplanting a pancreas was still considered an experimental procedure. Dee's nephrologist cautioned her against the risky surgery, but she felt convinced that it was her only hope for long-term survival. Without a functioning pancreas, Dee would still have diabetes, and her transplanted kidney would eventually fail again. Where would that leave her? After talking to other people who'd survived the surgery and researching her odds, she decided to go ahead.

"To me, it got to the point then that it felt like the only option," Dee tells me. She felt uncomfortable about praying for the organs, because someone would have to die for her to receive them, but she did pray that when the organs arrived, they would be accepted by her body. And they were. Except for one early rejection scare, Dee's new kidney and pancreas have worked perfectly.

Dee views the success of her transplants as a miracle, a gift from God. She feels that she owes the organ donor and his or her family her life. "Whenever I think about those miraculous, life-giving organs that were donated to me, it is overwhelming," Dee says, tearing up. "The fact that I was facing imminent death and was then given life again. I was reborn."

With the new organs working in her body, Dee worked to heal, focusing her attention on doing everything she could to help her body adjust to major physical changes. She hasn't needed insulin since her pancreas transplant, but trading that one medicine for a squadron of anti-rejection medications was a rocky adjustment.

Dee likes to be familiar with everything she puts into her body. When her new post-transplant medications were introduced, she felt overwhelmed by the sheer number of them.

One time, not long after her transplant, Jean was visiting Dee in the hospital. She was trying to help her friend sort her pills, when Dee threw the pills across the room. "She yelled, 'I am not going to take these anymore,'" Jean says. "I yelled back, 'Yes, you are,' and we both just started laughing. Then we had to pick up all those pills and start over again. But that moment was absolutely great. Dee needed to get it out. So did I. After that, things started looking up again, and Dee's attitude slowly started shifting back to normal. "

Out there on my own

For a young person, living with a serious chronic illness can feel isolating, like everyone else you know is walking around healthy and oblivious of their own mortality that chronically ill people must always look and act sick. That nagging feeling of isolation, like she was the only person out there living—and thriving—with type 1 diabetes, was what led Kerri Sparling to start her blog *Six Until Me*.

Diagnosed with type 1 diabetes in 1986 when she was just six years old, Sparling grew up with the reality of glucose monitoring, dietary restrictions, and frequent insulin injections (as many as nine a day before she decided to switch to an implanted insulin pump). She didn't know very many other people with diabetes—unless you counted the other kids at her beloved "diabetes camp," where all the counselors and campers had diabetes.

"There was something cool about mornings at camp when the nurse wheeled the cart of needles and syringes into the cabin and we'd all shoot up together," Sparling says. "There was this awesome sense of camaraderie at camp that I didn't have anywhere else."

As she grew older, and moved away from her parents and out into the world, there were times when Sparling felt that her chronic disease created an invisible wall around her. In college, the serious health implications of diabetes made Sparling more cautious than her peers. She needed to make sure she got enough sleep, ate well, and kept up on her meds.

"Young people with chronic illness don't go through that immortality phase that other young people go through," Sparling says. "We understand sooner than other kids that all of our lives are finite." She takes a breath and then laughs, remembering. "But then you go off to college and you don't want to do the whole diabetes thing. You want to focus on your studies. You want to go out and party and get laid and have a couple of drinks. You think you just want to be 'normal,' to hang out with the 'normal' kids, that you don't want to get involved with people with diabetes."

But by the time she graduated from college, married, and was making her way in the real world, Sparling felt ready to seek out other people with her disease. Though her (nondiabetic) husband was understanding, supportive, and kind, Sparling wanted more of those diabetes-camp style "Kumbaya" moments, where she could hang out with a group of other people living with the disease, sharing survival strategies, inside jokes, and stories of hope.

Online, the only information Sparling could find about her disease was grim. When she typed the word "diabetes" into Google, "you'd get lists of the ways you would die," she tells me, sighing. Sparling is a naturally funny and slyly positive person, so this was hard medicine to swallow. "I kept reading about people who were dying from diabetes or suffering from all these horrible complications. That was hard for me to see, and I knew there had to be other people out there like me. I just needed to find them."

Sparling's husband suggested that she start a blog to help get her story out to the general public, to provide hope for other people coping with type 1 diabetes and its side effects. So she started Six Until Me, named for the disease itself and the six years she lived until it came into her life. Within hours of her first posting, Sparling had connected with another person just like herself, a mostly healthy, youngish woman living with type 1 diabetes. Finding someone else out there was important, Sparling says to me, because she knew if there was one other person living a healthy life with the disease, there must be others, and then her future didn't seem quite so hopeless.

"You hear the diabetes horror stories," Sparling says, but she— with her fit, healthy appearance and vigorous way of living—fit into the ambiguous gray area of "hidden disability." From the outside, she didn't look like she was dealing with a chronic illness nearly every moment of her day. "So," Sparling continues, "you blend in and nobody gives a crap about you. But inside you are sick sometimes. The only people who understand are the people who are going through the same thing." Her blog, which she now maintains full time with the help of an editorial assistant, filled a need. Six Until Me's readership quickly grew to the tens of thousands, and other voices began to fill the virtual airwaves.

"When I started, there were maybe five people out there writing about this topic," Sparling says. "Now there are close to 1,000 people sharing their stories about life with diabetes through blogs and Tumblr and Twitter. It's amazing, a true victory of social media."

Double-dare

Sparling has always nurtured an inner badass, a "you can't tell me I can't do this" attitude that she feels provides some of the fuel that keeps her up and running even when coping with her disease can get exhausting. One of the things she had always been determined to do, even when others advised her against it, was give birth to a child.

"I've always wanted to be a mother," she says. But women with diabetes are considered high risk for pregnancies. A pregnant woman's blood sugars must be maintained at a stable level. High glucose levels can be harmful to a fetus, and existing symptoms of diabetes in the mother, including eye, kidney, or heart problems, are sometimes worsened during pregnancy. But, with care and planning, many women with diabetes have healthy pregnancies. Sparling had met quite a few through her blog. She was determined to be one of them.

Like many mothers with diabetes, Sparling is angered by the movie Steel Magnolias, where Julia Roberts' character, a new mother living with type 1 diabetes, dies from a diabetic reaction. Just talking about the scene in the movie makes Sparling exasperated. "That's what I was raised to think would happen if I ever had a child, but when somebody tells me I can't do something, my attitude is 'You can't tell me what to do.' When somebody puts that challenge out to me, it makes me want it even more. It made me fight harder to become a mother. And when my daughter was born, when I made it through my pregnancy, I wasn't giving Julia Roberts the finger exactly, but it did feel like I had won a victory."

If it seems like we've jumped ahead in the story, past the husband to the baby, that's the way Sparling likes to tell it. "I love my husband like crazy," she laughs, "but I wanted the baby more than the wedding."

Sparling met her husband through work. He learned about her diabetes early in the relationship, but not the way she planned it would happen. It's a "meet cute" moment, with an amusing chronic-illness twist.

"I was trying to chat him up," Sparling recalls, laughing. "I wanted him to think I was cute. My insulin pump was clipped to the waistband of my pants, and I was reaching for something near him, trying to get closer." In the reaching, Sparling's shirt hiked up a bit, and her pump was exposed. "At first he thought I was wearing a beeper," she laughs again, relishing the opportunity to tell the story. "Then he realized it was an insulin pump. One of his friends had a girlfriend with an insulin pump, so he knew what they looked like. He said to me, flirty-like, 'I see you have an insulin pump.' I still think that's hilarious."

Sparling always makes a point of getting the fact that she has diabetes out in the open right away—and when she was single, that was especially true when it came to potential romantic partners.

"When it came to dating, diabetes was a good barometer for assholes," she says. "If you are not cool with it, it's like hating my mom. For me, it's a deal breaker."

Sparling says she doesn't blame people for being concerned about entering into a relationship with someone with a serious chronic illness. But she also doesn't get herself worked up about their reactions. "It's not your fault if you can't handle it," she says, plainly, "but it's not my problem, either."

The success of Six Until Me has turned Sparling into a sort of diabetes "celebrity spokesperson." She speaks at conferences, to physicians, patients, and pharmaceutical executives, talking about her experience living a normal, everyday life with type 1 diabetes and reviewing the different drugs and medical devices that have been developed to treat the disease.

She likes to think that her blog helped build a community of individuals living with diabetes, people who don't define themselves as patients but rather as people. Sparling wants her story—and the stories of other people with diabetes—to get out into the world and break down some of those invisible walls of silence.

That said, Sparling doesn't feel all that comfortable with the description of "diabetes activist." "I see myself more as a storyteller," she says. "Type 1 diabetes is a story that needs to be told. There is a stigma attached to this condition. I wanted people to know what it is really like."

And *living* with diabetes is key for Sparling. While she doesn't hold out hope for a cure, she does think that giving the disease a human face will help spur more research and innovation to help improve her life and the lives of other people in her situation.

"When I was diagnosed in 1986, they told my mom that the diabetes would cut my life short by eight to twenty-two years," Sparling says.

Thanks to the efforts of people like Sparling, life expectancy for people with type 1 diabetes has improved significantly in the last decade. Ever the survivor, she likes to turn what used to feel like bad news into a reason to live the life she's been given in the best way she knows how. "If you think you are going to die when you're sixty, you'd better make it an awesome sixty years," Sparling says.

The road to resilience: Joe Nelson

Joe Nelson, a psychologist in private practice, grew up in the "bad old days" of diabetes treatment, well before the development of glucose monitors or insulin pumps, and when his diabetic father's blood sugars fluctuated, alarm bells went off for every member of his family.

"Back then, growing up with a father with type 1 diabetes was terrifying," Nelson, sixty-two, tells me. "There was no patient or family education, so we didn't understand how it worked. We didn't really know how to prevent anything, so if my dad started to have an insulin reaction, we just had to react. My job was to get out the orange juice, and mix a bunch of sugar in it and try to help my mom feed it to him. Sometimes, he'd be belligerent. Sometimes he'd be silly and laughing and having fun. Sometimes he'd be convulsing. As a kid, all I knew was that I didn't want to get to the point where he was convulsing. I didn't want him to die."

On average, Nelson's father would have at least one reaction a week. The unpredictability, combined with the lack of education or support, caused great stress for him and his mother. "At that time, there was nobody interested in talking about diabetes, much less its impact on family members," Nelson tells me. His experience led to his career counseling families and individuals dealing with diabetes and other chronic illness. He's also on the editorial board of the American Association of Diabetes Educators' journal AADE Practice.

During his decades in practice, Nelson has studied resilience in people with chronic illness. Some of his clients, when faced with seemingly insurmountable health challenges similar to those Dee deals with every day, rise to the occasion and "set a place for diabetes or chronic illness at their table," he says, continuing to live regular, high-quality lives. Others create—or accept—a list of limitations for themselves, framing themselves as victims of their health and building a life that sets limits rather than expanding opportunities.

Nelson has found that there are different levels of resilience. Over the years, he's observed the many ways his clients cope with serious health challenges—either for themselves or their loved ones. Some, like Dee or Kerri Sparling, rebound from challenges, ready to welcome the new day. Others struggle to find meaning in lives they consider to be diminished.

Through his interactions with his clients, Nelson tries to understand what it takes to wrap your arms around trauma and challenge—especially when the trauma and challenge is chronic and may never go away.

"I worked with a man who, when he first came in, was having frequent insulin reactions that were freaking his family out and causing his wife a lot of distress," Nelson tells me. "He was so uncomfortable with the fact that he had diabetes that he wouldn't report it to anybody. He had a lot of shame about it."

Nelson and his client worked together to discuss treatment

options and lifestyle adjustments that the man could make to build diabetes treatment into his regular life. Once the client realized that diabetes didn't have to take over his life, he began to have more peace about it. This was helpful in his treatment and recovery. "When he finally got to a place where he could have some sense of acceptance about having diabetes as part of his life, when he found that it was acceptable that he might have some help, his diabetes improved dramatically. The incidents he was having almost disappeared."

Nelson believes that while some of the attitudes that aid resilience can be taught, much of the strength that it takes to face serious life challenges is inborn and must be nurtured and encouraged.

"The truth is, we all end up at some point in our lives being a victim of something, so people who constantly perceive themselves as victims or suffering at the whim of the world are the very people who are going to struggle the most," Nelson says. "They don't believe that they have direct control over what they are going to do. They want direction on how to move, but the only way they are going to learn to move is on their own. The discovery process of them finding out they are not a victim is a long, interesting struggle."

Nelson tells me that he has a long history with a client who struggles to keep her serious physical limitations from becoming serious emotional limitations.

"This woman has been my client for twenty-five years," Nelson reports. "She comes in once every ten days. She's somebody who has had multiple health problems with her diabetes. She's had visual issues. She's had a kidney transplant, a heart bypass. She's a bilateral amputee." She's not the most inspiring, high-energy person, Nelson says, but this woman is doing her best to get by, to try to live her life in the best way she can. "I don't know that I would term her as someone who's resilient, exactly," he says, "but she hasn't killed herself, either. She continues to live a life."

Resilience in the face of serious chronic illness doesn't always resemble sainthood, like Dee's, Nelson says. And it doesn't always look like sassy advocacy like Sparling's. Sometimes resilience looks more like one foot in front of the other.

"There are some things about this woman that resemble resilience without her being the kind of person who puts on spring legs and runs a race," he says. "She's still strong, in her own way."

From Nelson's perspective, another portrait of resilience is the client who first denied the existence of his disease until health problems—combined with family pressure—forced him to open up about his struggles.

"I think in his own way he was very resilient, very positive in his perspective," Nelson says. "He never believed that diabetes was going to get him. Instead, he was going to get diabetes. Even though he experienced the shame about it, he made a shift in his perspective, saying, 'I am not defined by this disease.' As much as at first he didn't want to admit that disease was part of his life, eventually he decided to think that he was still a whole person, that his disease wasn't defining him."

And Nelson doesn't credit himself with his client's transformation. "I hung around the guy long enough and offered him some ideas that helped him shift some of his thinking," he says. "Then on his own he became ready to be able to see things differently. He always had the positivity. He always had the feeling that things were going to improve no matter what. He came to the sessions with that perspective that life could be better. He made a huge attitude shift, and he did it himself."

With some clients, Nelson takes his victories where he can get them. "This woman I've seen for twenty-five years is finally at a place where she felt she could be confident enough to take a driving class," he says. "That was a major victory for her. I'm hoping she's going to build on that confidence in the rest of her life."

Even though resilience may be inborn, it sometimes takes time to uncover, Nelson says. Like a rough stone washed up on the shore, a good wash and polish uncovers startling beauty.

"Early on I worked with a man with severe diabetes," Nelson says. "When I met him, he was blind. He was simply just sitting there alone in his apartment. I would go over and visit him and he was depressed so we worked with his depression first, his self-talk that kept him in that stuck place. Somewhere, deep inside, this man had this strong core. As he came out of his depression, he found a job working in a hospital as a cook."

The cooking job introduced Nelson's client to a world outside his lonely apartment.

"He found a club of blind people who would do things like ski," Nelson says, clearly still amazed at the story. "He would go skiing with them. He'd go out and do events with them. He became active and was enjoying his life. He was on dialysis, eventually had a kidney transplant but then had a heart attack and died. It was tragic, but he truly lived the rest of his life."

Over his years of practice, Nelson has come to believe that chronic illness or other life challenges don't always have to be looked on as a burden. He tries to encourage his clients to look at the challenges that shape their lives through a different lens, to uncover the wisdom or insight that those challenges bring.

Nelson is particularly drawn to "The Guest House," a poem written by Rumi, a thirteenth-century Persian poet and mystic.

"The poem describes how we can either try to push away the stuff that worries and terrifies us or we can get closer to it," he says to me. "We can invite it in. By trying to get rid of our challenges, we really give up control. We give up our impact. But if we invite those challenges and traumas in and get to accept and know them, we are clearing the way for other possibilities."

The Guest House by Rumi

This being human is a guest house.
Every morning a new arrival.

A joy, a depression, a meanness,
some momentary awareness comes
As an unexpected visitor.

Welcome and entertain them all!
Even if they're a crowd of sorrows,

who violently sweep your house
empty of its furniture,
still treat each guest honorably.
He may be clearing you out
for some new delight.

The dark thought, the shame, the malice,
meet them at the door laughing,
and invite them in.

Be grateful for whoever comes,
because each has been sent
as a guide from beyond.

In her own way, Dee has treated chronic illness as a guest in her house. While there have been days when she wishes her illness would go away and leave her alone, she also has a strange appreciation for the gifts it has given her, gifts of humility, patience, thankfulness, and faith. These are gifts Dee's not sure she'd have in such abundance if she'd lived a normal, healthy life.

"If I could ask for anything, I don't know if I'd ask to have my illness taken away," she tells me. "In a way, it's been a gift to me. It makes me really see and appreciate all the good things about the world that have been set in front of me. If I were perfect, I don't know if I'd really appreciate the greatness of all the individual small things I've been given."

Survival tips for the chronically ill from people who've been there:

✚ Live for each day, Dee says. Don't dwell on the past or worry about the future.

"It doesn't make sense for me to live my life fretting over what happened yesterday or what could happen to my health tomorrow," she says. "All I have is right now, and every day is a bright, new opportunity."

+ To survive long term with serious chronic illness, **Dee suggests listening to your body—but also listening to doctors' advice**. She advises others living with chronic illness to understand their own subtle physical cues, and react to them, but she also believes strongly in following her physicians' orders—to the letter.

"That's what doctors are paid for," Dee says. "It's their job to keep me alive, so I usually do everything they tell me to do. It's worked this long."

+ **Nobody can be perfect all the time**. Dee advises forgiving yourself for days when you are not perfect. "Don't try to be perfect every day," she says. "When you've got a bunch of health challenges like I do, there are going to be some days where you'd rather not smile all the time." If you get angry, get over it, Dee says. Accept your humanity— and expect that your loved ones will, too.

+ **Practice prayer, thankfulness and faith in a higher power**, Dee says.

"God has helped me through everything," she says. "He's my power source."

+ Kerri Sparling says it's important to **find your people**.

"Until I started my blog, there were times when I felt so very alone," she says, "but once I put myself out there and discovered a whole world of other people like me, it was a true revelation. It made living with my disease a whole lot easier."

+ **Don't listen to the naysayers**, Sparling says. If someone sets limitations because of your illness, find a way around them.

"One of the things that gives me energy is that 'screw you' feeling I get when someone says something like 'A person with type 1 diabetes can't do this,'" she says. "My response is, 'Don't tell me what I *can't* do with my disease. If I want to do something, I'll find out a way to do it *despite* my disease.'"

+ When telling others about your disease, **be upfront, positive and proud**, Sparling advises.

"It's all in the messaging," she laughs. A big part about how people perceive chronic illnesses is through their interactions with people who live with them. "If I am open and honest about my diabetes while remaining positive about the quality of my life, other people won't feel sorry for me. And if they don't feel sorry for me, I don't feel sorry for myself."

+ **Try looking at your chronic illness as a source of wisdom and insight, rather than a burden,** psychologist Joe Nelson says. This is a tough accomplishment, he says, but it is one that he feels is worth the effort for everyone.

"For many people, this attitude shift requires a major adjustment," Nelson says, "but it's also a true eye-opener and life-enhancer. And realizing the wisdom that comes from chronic illness opens a person up for greater resiliency."

Chapter 4
How to Survive a Partner's Seismic Change

Sure, prenuptial agreements exist, and some people refuse to enter into a committed relationship before agreeing to a pre-arranged set of expectations. Are children required? Will both partners remain employed and contribute to the family coffers? What about infidelity? Or illness? What will happen to assets if the pair ultimately decides to split? Theoretically, it seems, there are legal ways to plan ahead in a relationship, to protect oneself from heartbreak, betrayal, or, simply, the unexpected.

But that doesn't sound very romantic, does it? Most of us are far less practical when it comes to love. We are drawn to one person—physically, emotionally, intellectually—and, eventually, we decide to become a pair of individuals committed to one another.

Most couples talk before committing, sketching out plans for the future, goals and dreams that both members can agree on. But no one can really predict and plan for the future. And who would want to, anyway? I started dating my husband four months into our first year in college; by the time we married at age 24, I felt like I knew him better than anyone else in the world. We'd talked about everything, or so it seemed, and though we never even considered drawing up a document that quantified a list of deal breakers in our marriage, I think we both felt confident that we had the same goals for our life together.

One of the unspoken goals in our marriage was children. But because we'd married so young, in the beginning having a family seemed years away. And it was. As my late twenties loomed, and as I watched my neighbors and co-workers breed baby after baby, part of me started to rethink the idea of parenthood. I was enjoying my career, loving life with our still-childless friends, and relishing the unencumbered freedom of being two working adults with no children. I remember reading a spunky, defiant essay written by an intentionally child-free woman, and the description of her unencumbered life appealed to me. Perhaps that was the way I wanted to live my life.

One Sunday afternoon, driving home from a weekend trip, I tried out the idea on my husband. I talked about how I loved the life we had together, how I worried that children would ruin my career, alter our relationship, distance us from our friends.

Though we'd never officially agreed to procreate, my shift in attitude left my husband feeling blindsided. Creating a family (and, to him, that meant parenting children) was something he'd always assumed would be an essential part of our marriage. Here I was, in one car ride, changing everything.

"If you don't want to have children," he told me, clenching his jaw, "I want to find another way to be a father." He wasn't saying he wanted out of our marriage, but he was saying he wanted to be a father.

We had a friend whose lesbian sister and her partner had asked him to be a sperm donor; we also knew a young man in college who made extra money by making donations at a local sperm bank. After my husband spoke, I realized that on some base level, the idea of someone else carrying his child made me feel sick to my stomach. I couldn't imagine this happening. The truth is that I'd always felt a biological desire to someday conceive this man's children, a desire I'd buried under other ambitions and careful plans. And so, a few years and several long conversations later, we set out to make our first baby.

In the end, I came to the idea of being a mother on my own. And by the time our first daughter was conceived, it felt like I wanted her more than anyone else in the world. But if I'm being honest with myself, I know it was my husband's desire for fatherhood—and my deep love for him—that sent me down the road to motherhood. When I first voiced my ambiguity about having children, he felt like I was suddenly changing the road map for our future. Luckily for our partnership, I changed my mind—and he gave me the space I needed to make that change.

It's impossible—and unhealthy—to plan ahead for all contingencies before entering into a committed relationship, says Karen Gail Lewis, a couples therapist and author based in Washington, D.C., and Cincinnati. "There are too many possible scenarios," she says. And mapping out all the changes that could happen in a lifetime could scare a person away from long-term love.

Martin Novell, a marriage and family therapist based in West Los Angeles, says that the secret to maintaining a healthy long-term relationship is cultivating a willingness to ride out change. Of course, there are times when a partner changes so drastically that the relationship cannot continue, but in many cases riding out the storm of change requires patience, love, and understanding. My husband had all three in abundant supply.

In a case of one partner undergoing a major change, Novell says, both members need to ask themselves, "'What kind of cargo is this ship carrying?' What sort of strength, loyalty, and commitment do we have for one another? What is our history of loyalty?' Part of being in a successful relationship is being a witness to each other's changes and newness. Change is a part of growth." Face it, Novell says. "You don't really want to be married to a person who is the same as they were when you married them at age twenty when they are age forty. Change can be good."

Never the same

Lynette tells me that her husband, Rob, changed forever the moment his "head blew up on our bathroom floor."

In a way, it wasn't as grisly as it sounds: Rob's head didn't actually *blow up*, at least not the outside of his head, but gray matter inside did explode when a blood clot burst in his brain, causing heavy internal bleeding and a massive stroke.

Rob was in his mid-forties at the time of his stroke. He was outwardly healthy, an active, intelligent man, a successful architect who didn't smoke, had a healthy heart, and wasn't overweight. Lynette was hours away, returning from a visit to her ailing mother, when the stroke occurred; Rob was home with their two daughters, ages six and ten.

Rob had been mediating an everyday argument between the sisters when he collapsed. Because he wasn't bleeding on the outside and just looked like he had suddenly fallen asleep, the girls didn't call an ambulance. Instead, they tried calling their mother, but she had turned her cell phone off for the drive home. When Lynette pulled her car into the driveway, the girls greeted her, laughing, saying, "Come upstairs. Dad is playing a game."

Lynette is a writer, and she described what happened next in an essay she wrote titled "Strokeland":

> What I see in the bathroom isn't funny. Rob is lying on the floor in the fetal position, twitching, unconscious. Dad started to fall when we were fighting, Grace tells me. She's 10. We helped him lie down. We gave him a pillow . . . We rode our bikes around the block. I had Julia watch a movie. He was talking funny.
>
> I start to yell, Get a phone. Call 911. Where's the phone? I run downstairs and make a call I can no longer remember.
>
> Soon the EMTs are charging upstairs, asking questions I can't answer. The worst one is, How long has he been lying there? The girls don't know. They ask me again in the emergency room when they tell me it's a stroke. It's been hours since he dropped, and now that magic window for clawing out the clot could be closed. There was no blood, so the kids didn't call. I can't think straight but I do know this: I must always tell them it wasn't their fault. They took care of him the best they could.

Rob survived his stroke, but it left him a changed man. In the years since the incident, he's made amazing strides. He can walk around the lake near their home; talk, albeit slowly; drive; and cook dinner. But his brain injury has left him unable to keep up with

Lynette's witty banter and active mind. Too much activity tires him and he has to go to bed early. He will never again be able to work as an architect. During the day, Rob stays at home while Lynette is at work and their daughters are at school.

Lynette tells me that Rob's stroke not only changed him, it changed their marriage. She explains that she was first drawn to her husband because of his personality. She had been married briefly once before, to a man who was emotionally abusive, and Rob, with his gentle heart, sharp brain, and wry sense of humor, felt like a perfect match. Their courtship was brief, and when they decided to marry, they did so with the speed of experienced adults certain they had found the ideal partner.

"Looking back—and I think this is so true of a lot of marriages—we've always had more of an intellectual connection than a physical connection," Lynette says. "We do have a lot in common. Rob is really smart and interesting. We were both really ready to get married when we found each other. We had both had a lot of relationships and wanted to settle down."

At first, after the stroke, it wasn't clear if Rob would live. But after his condition stabilized and he left the hospital for a rehab center and eventually home, Lynette grew frustrated with people's assumption that one day he would magically be back to normal.

For the majority of stroke sufferers, it doesn't work that way. Two weeks after Rob's stroke, Lynette recalls that a doctor took her aside. "He said," she says, "'Professionals with this kind of brain damage just don't go back to work.'" She sighs at the memory. "Hearing that was hard, of course, but taking it in and then repeating it to other people really helped me cope. I think because it helped me let go of that piece of hoping for complete recovery and think, 'OK. What's next? This is gone. Move on.' If people don't hear that, they live in a fantasyland and in the end, when things don't go back to how they were before the stroke, they have more pain. I like to face reality."

Talking to others and being open about her emotions is the way Lynette deals with trauma. When her first marriage imploded, she turned to her massive network of friends for love and support. When she dated an alcoholic, she joined Al-Anon. When she and

Rob discovered that they could not have biological children, she got involved with the local chapter of Resolve, an infertility support group.

After Rob's stroke, Lynette joined a support group for caregivers of people who'd had strokes. Unlike her earlier experiences, this group did not provide the support that Lynette was seeking. She and Rob were in their forties when he had his stroke. Most people who have strokes are much older, and Lynette found herself surrounded by women closer to her mother's age.

"Their issues were completely different than mine," she says. "I still had young kids. They had grandchildren."

This lack of obvious support left Lynette feeling frustrated and alone, an odd, discomforting feeling for an extrovert. She talked to friends and relatives about her feelings, but they didn't really understand. She met with a therapist, and while that helped, she still craved conversations with others who had lived through a similar situation. So she sat down at her computer and began writing about her experiences. One of her essays, responding to public expectations surrounding Arizona Congresswoman Gabrielle Gifford's traumatic brain injury, was published in her city's daily newspaper.

"My op-ed was about how people with major brain incidents and strokes usually don't recover enough to go back to work," Lynette tells me. "After it was published, I got a number of e-mails and calls from women whose husbands had had strokes. They had read my editorial or knew someone who had read it. I invited them all out to coffee."

In rapid fashion, a support group was formed. "The women who contacted me were glad that I said what I'd said because they knew like I did that people just can't accept that a forty- or fifty-year-old person is done working after they have a stroke," Lynette says. "At the coffee, there were five of us, plus five other women I had invited. They all wanted to be in a support setting with middle-aged women, because so many people who have strokes are much older, and that's who's usually at the official support groups. I think my essay struck a nerve."

The group began meeting regularly, and at the beginning it felt like a balm for Lynette to meet with a group of women who understood what she was going through.

"I like being somewhere with people who know what I mean when I talk about that blank look my husband has in his eyes or the frustration of doing everything by myself," she says. But after a few meetings it became clear to Lynette that her new friends weren't willing to take the next step, to move beyond the role of caregiver and allow themselves to feel angry or frustrated that their husbands are no longer the same man they married.

"Ultimately I've been frustrated by this group because I keep wanting to fight against the parameters of my situation," Lynette says, "whether that means I hire a nanny so I can get out or I volunteer at a nonprofit so I can be out in the world and travel. Most of the women I've met play more of a martyr or victim role. They like the parameters, and if you suggest alternatives, they just always shut it down. This one woman told me she thinks someone has to be in her house 24/7 and I said, 'Why don't you get him a Lifeline? Or have someone come in and take care of him?' and she says, 'No, no.' There's just a feeling that these women are so upset and depressed and helpless. It starts to bug and depress me to be around them. I want to be active and make things better."

Not long after Lynette's husband had his stroke, her therapist suggested she divorce him—or at least move him into a nearby apartment. She told friends that she was considering making the move. The idea made most people extremely uncomfortable.

"I think that maybe the fact that I actually thought about these options, that I needed to play with the idea and ultimately reject it is pretty threatening for people," Lynette says now. She looks at me with steady blue eyes. "I don't think they even want to go there, really. It's scary." She even brought up the idea in her ad hoc stroke caregivers' support group.

"It really shut down the dinner when I brought that up," Lynette says. "I said, 'Have you thought about having an affair? Not just for the sex part but for the lonely part.' They all looked at me with these shocked faces. And Rob is one of the husbands in the best shape. One of the guys in the group, he can't talk at all. He just kind of babbles. I mean Jesus. At least my husband can talk a little bit. But this particular group of women just doesn't want to go there."

Lynette thinks the idea of leaving an ailing spouse is a taboo subject for women. Men, she says, are more likely to leave a spouse when she becomes severely disabled. "If I were the one who had the stroke," she says, slowly, "I think a lot of people would support Rob if he decided to move on. I think we think men just don't have the natural nurturing qualities needed to care for a sick spouse."

Unexpected disability is a major stressor in relationships, therapist Martin Novell says. Even though they usually hear the words "in sickness and in health," no one likes to imagine their partner transformed by an ailment into someone completely different from who they were when they fell in love. Among his many clients is a couple where the wife was diagnosed with a severe form of multiple sclerosis and eventually needed to use a wheelchair. The couple's relationship was faltering, Novell recalls, in part because of the husband's frustration at having to take care of his wife's needs. The wife felt guilty about having to ask so much of her husband. Another side of her also felt angry about his resentment.

The husband, Novell says, "couldn't express how uncomfortable he was at having to get up at three in the morning to help his wife go to the bathroom. He felt like he couldn't express the anger he had about having a wife who really couldn't move. He couldn't express the difficulty he had with having to help her all the time."

In their sessions, he was able to help the husband and wife talk to each other about their feelings. Over time, they were able to develop a deeper understanding of each other's situations. They began to see each other as full human beings again, not as "sick person" and "caregiver." They were able to uncover the love that had brought them together in the first place.

"In this couple," Novell says, "it turns out they were able to realize the resilience they had in their partnership. It turned out they had the strength they needed to remain together and be happy. It is a therapist's job to help uncover that inner strength."

Novell tells me that he advises couples that have gone through a traumatic change to give themselves and their relationship time to adjust before they make big changes.

"There's a process and the journey toward making a big, final decision," he says. "It's important to gather all the information. Things usually look quite bleak at the beginning of this type of trauma. You are as overwhelmed and traumatized as the partner who actually went through the change. It is not a time to change your life any more than it's already been changed. Instead, it is a time to learn how to make decisions. It is a time to use the resources of the community, including therapy, a medical doctor, someplace where you can get a third opinion, a support group. These are the kinds of places where you can get information to help you process this change and find out what it means to you."

Relationship therapist Karen Gail Lewis has worked with many couples facing the trauma of one partner's significant disability. Often in these cases, caregivers struggle when their feelings of guilt and anger get twisted up together, she says. What's left is a tangle of unresolved emotions.

"Sometimes clients will say they feel guilty for being angry at their partner for changing—even though they know they did nothing to bring on their illness or injury," Lewis says. "I assure them that those feelings are perfectly normal. But I do try to help separate out the guilt from the anger. I try to normalize the guilt and give them an opening to express a full range of emotions."

This work often leads people to admit, angrily, "This situation is not fair to me." In those cases, Lewis says that she tells her clients, "You have every reason to be angry about what happened. You have every reason to be furious. Your whole life was turned around in a second." After those emotions have been expressed, Lewis says, she works with her clients on moving forward, on building a new relationship from the pieces that exist. "I assure them that the anger is natural, though it is something that can eventually be dissolved."

It's a hard reality to grasp, especially when a change occurs in an instant. But, Lewis says, change is a central part of life. Unlike fairy tales, real human lives are forever shifting, changing.

"I don't think 'happily ever after' exists for anyone," Lewis says. "'Ever after' sounds eternal." The truth is, nobody ever lives *ever after*, she tells me. Couples who are in it for the long haul need to accept change and grow from it. They need to uncover what's good about the change.

Lynette says that as the years have passed since Rob's stroke, things have gotten easier in their marriage. While she still deeply misses the man she married, she does appreciate many things about the man Rob has become. Their relationship, much like any relationship, is a work in progress. It takes time and concentration to keep it healthy. And, Lynette has realized, appreciating what still exists in their partnership requires her to look at life from a different perspective.

"One thing that has helped our marriage is to say, 'What's the good part that's still left?'" she says. "We still have fun sitting around the dining room table with four of us having dinner and talking. We still have fun on vacation. And my husband is still there parenting. It's good to step back and say, 'What are the good things that are still there?' and not focus on 'He can't design houses anymore.'" That sort of thought just leaves her lingering in the past rather than living in the present.

Post-stroke, Rob—formerly cautious and conservative with money—now encourages Lynette to go on adventures. She appreciates his unwavering support of her many solo journeys, and hopes this hard-won perspective will someday rub off on their daughters.

"Now," Lynette smiles, "Rob says, 'Don't hold back. If you want to go somewhere, go somewhere.' He has a great attitude. He says it to everyone. He says it to our nannies. He's like, 'Take that trip to Europe even if you have to borrow money, because you never know what might happen in the future.' And 'Don't live your life for your retirement.' Before the stroke, we fought about money because I would want to go on trips and he didn't want to overspend. I was much more 'Embrace the day.' Now, since the stroke, he would say, 'I wish I would've done more when I could.' People often think that when they are older, but they don't usually get there at forty-five like Rob did."

Not so long ago, Lynette took a writing class focused on personal essays. (It's where she wrote "Strokeland," the essay quoted above.) As is her inclination, Lynette soaked in her classmates' stories, quickly making friends and connecting with her fellow writers. As the class progressed, and people began reading their essays out loud, she realized that every member of this diverse group had some trauma they were wrestling with. For Lynette, that realization was comforting.

"You look around the first day of class and everybody looks spunky and healthy," she says, "and then you learn that one young woman's mom killed herself when she was fifty-seven and the other was raped and the other's dad was an alcoholic. You realize that everybody's got some pain they're walking around with, and yeah, what happened to my husband is shocking and hard, but it's not as bad as having a kid who's still in diapers at twelve or can't move. There are so many worse things."

So while Rob will never be the man he was before the stroke permanently damaged his brain, Lynette believes that with the help of others, he—and she—have slowly come around to an acceptance of the life they are living now. And despite the challenges, on most days, they both continue to thrive.

"I think my husband would give his life a pretty high grade," Lynette tells me one day over lunch. "He really enjoys just being at home with the animals and the kids, and he likes to ride his bike and go for walks, and whenever we go on any kind of trip he just loves that. He reads a lot. He just enjoys everything—even just going to a movie. Before the stroke, his style of parenting used to be more about trying to mold and shape and scold the girls. Now he just much more appreciates everything that's funny or interesting about being a father. He revels in it."

As for herself, Lynette still has her dark days, times—like in her self-created support group—where she rages against the walls and restrictions her fellow "stroke wives" put up for themselves. But she also feels a certain sense of pride in the open, up-front way she has chosen to live her life. Her writing helps her put her feelings into words and reveal truths for others. Her life, while not the one she expected when she married, still remains good—and well worth living.

A chance match

After spending twenty years tangled in a painful and disappointing first marriage, Carol couldn't believe her luck when she met Bill, a tall, witty, and charming musician.

"I was divorcing," she says. "My divorce was just about final. A friend invited me to a party at her house. I didn't want to go, but she persuaded me and I went. There was Billy. I thought he was so handsome and smart."

Carol, a poet and mother of eight, was enchanted by Bill. He, too, was in the process of a divorce. ("He was sort of brokenhearted," Carol recalls, and adds with a laugh, "I wasn't brokenhearted at all.") The two so enjoyed their first conversation that they agreed to meet again. And again. Quickly, they were smitten. And then they were a couple.

"Right away, in those first months, I knew he was the one for me," Carol says, and, behind her round, black-framed glasses, her eyes flash at the memory. Before long, she was introducing Bill to her children. Hungry for a strong father figure, they appreciated Bill's old-fashioned-but-loving style. When he moved in with Carol and her two youngest children, it felt natural. Bill, she recalls, was a wonderful, supportive father figure and friend. "The best father they ever had."

Carol and Bill never married, but they had been happily living together for years, forming their own kind of family unit, when everything changed.

"Bill was doing a favor for a friend of mine," Carol, now seventy-nine, recalls. "He had driven her car to New York. He was in the city visiting his family for maybe four hours. He was crossing Third Avenue when he was hit by a car." It was a hit and run.

"Bill was a big guy," Carol says. "The driver jumped the light, hit him in the legs, and he flew up in the air. Bill's head went through the guy's windshield. The driver pushed him out of his car, Bill's head hit the curb, and the driver drove off. A New York cabbie chased the guy down and pinned his car against a sanitary truck. The police arrested him."

Bill's injuries were extensive. At first, doctors talked about amputating his legs, but they managed to save them. He had broken bones and severely lacerated skin. But the most injured was Bill's brain.

"He was in the hospital for about a month," Carol tells me over coffee one crisply cool morning. "He was in a coma." Carol, who had flown to New York as soon as she heard about the accident, stayed by his side in the hospital. Friends and family also came to see him. Eventually, Bill emerged from the coma a changed man.

"He was there for sure," Carol says to me, slowly, "but he was gone, too. It's hard to explain, but he wasn't the same at all." When Bill was discharged from the hospital, Carol flew him home to Minnesota. For a time, Bill went to a rehabilitation institute, and then to a transitional nursing home. When it was clear he wasn't doing well in the nursing home, Carol decided to take Bill home to live with her. Bill couldn't drive. He couldn't work. He could barely read. Doctors told Carol that he shouldn't be left alone.

"I remember his doctors saying, 'You can't do this,'" Carol says, "but I took him home anyway. And then he really declined. I couldn't be home all the time and I could see he was miserable there when I was gone. He accidentally started a fire in the microwave. He moped around the apartment." Lost, confused, and unable to communicate his feelings, Bill retreated into an impenetrable silence. After much thought, Carol conceded that it wasn't wise for her to keep Bill at home. He would need to move into a long-term-care facility.

For Carol, this felt like a failure, and only added to her discouraged feelings about Bill's future. For months after the accident, she allowed herself to believe that maybe one day he'd return to his courtly, clever self, that his brain would miraculously heal and she would have her partner back. But, she eventually told herself, that would never happen. She would have to accept reality and learn to build a new life around that.

Partners for life

It took several months of trial and error, but once Bill was safely settled in a care facility that met his needs, Carol could very easily have cut off her visits and moved on. His short-term memory was shot, she says with a laugh. He'd probably never realize if she didn't show up. But that wasn't the way it went.

For the next fifteen years of his life, Bill lived in a care facility, and Carol visited or spoke to him nearly every day. Even though Bill was no longer the man she fell in love with, and even though she had no legal marriage ties to bind her to him, Carol insists she never considered turning her back on Bill.

"I certainly didn't sign up for what happened to him, but I never, ever thought of leaving him. He had been such a"—here she tears up and then quickly dries her eyes on a napkin—"huge contributor to my life and the lives of my children and he was such an excellent partner. No matter what happened in life he was always by my side. Now it was my turn to pay him back."

To cope with the sadness and stress around Bill's injuries, Carol turned to her family and friends. A poet and playwright, she also turned to words to regain her strength, writing poems about Bill and their time together. And she also turned to Bill.

Even though his brain didn't work the way it did before the accident, Carol went to Bill for advice and support for mundane and complex problems. "He was my best friend," she says, simply, "and even when he was brain-injured, if I had some problem, I would call him and he'd give me some resolution to the problem. What he said didn't always make sense, but it made me feel better. He remained a big, huge support." But it often wasn't easy spending time with Bill, she says. "He was so slow and bumbling. He'd annoy the hell out of me. Sometimes I'd get frustrated and ask him silly things like 'Can't you get dressed? Can't you talk?'"

A decade and a half after the hit-and-run, Bill died of natural causes. He was seventy years old. Carol was with Bill when he died.

"I went to see him on the night before," she recalls. "I said, 'I am going to leave now, but I will be back tomorrow.' And he said the first clear thing he had said in a month: 'And what exactly do you mean by that?'" she repeats, still amused at the memory. "The next day they called me and said his breathing was labored. I got right out there. He was nearly gone by the time I got there but I did hold his hand, which was still warm. And all my children came out there immediately when I called. We all stood around his bed and cried. I signed him up with the cremation society and they came with a great, big huge red-velvet sling, which he would've loved. He was so dramatic."

Looking back on the years of Bill's illness, Carol wants to make it clear that she felt that while she wouldn't wish the experience on anyone else, she still felt like something positive came out of that time. Of course, she missed the man she fell in love with, but, she believes, his essence remained, even when his actions were limited.

"I don't feel like I'd been cheated," Carol tells me. "I don't feel like caring for him was exhausting. He was my family. I would do for him what I would do for any family member. I believe we will be together forever after. He was this wonderful gift, this great friend to me."

It's not you. It's me.

Years before Randy married a woman, he knew that he was gay. When he was a young adult, he even considered coming out to his family, but he couldn't build up the courage.

Now in his mid-fifties, he has open, honest eyes, short salt-and-pepper hair and a neatly trimmed beard. "There were too many expectations of who I was going to be, what I was going to do. I didn't want to disappoint anyone."

This was back in the 1970s, Randy adds, and most people he knew saw being gay as some kind of personal failure. A high achiever who valued family connections, Randy felt certain that his parents and siblings would reject him if he admitted to loving men. He didn't think he could face life on his own.

"I asked myself," Randy says, "'Am I old enough, strong enough, independent enough to lose my family?' I knew I wasn't. I couldn't do that."

So Randy pushed his feelings for men aside. He married a woman and they had two children. For nearly seventeen years, Randy never told his wife that he was attracted to men. Instead, he told himself that these feelings were a weakness on his part, something that he needed to push aside in order to live the "normal" life that was expected of him. Randy still feels guilty about what living this lie did to his former spouse.

"I always knew I was gay, but the thing about it was that I willingly made the choice to get married to a woman," Randy says. He looks me square in the eye as he says this, though he shifts his body uncomfortably. "It's one of those things where you try to fool yourself. You say, 'I can do this.' And I did it for a long time. But it wasn't fair to anyone."

Then, when he was forty-five, Randy reached a tipping point.

"I got to a place in my life where I was having trouble living with myself," he says. "I was angry, restless. I didn't realize it at the time, but I think it was particularly hard to live with me then."

Randy says that his wife chalked his mood swings up to a midlife crisis. It may have been partly that, he supposes, but he also knew it was more. One night he had a dream that he remembers as a "horrible nightmare."

"I'm not the kind of person who usually remembers my dreams," Randy says. In the dream, "I was on my deathbed and all I could think was, 'I never got to live the life I wanted to live.'" Randy pauses, and looks down at his tea. "I was in a panic and there was nothing I could do about it. This dream got me in such a state that I woke up in a cold sweat. The sheets were soaked—the whole nine yards."

Randy tried to go back to sleep and put the dream out of his mind, but when he woke up in the morning, he couldn't shake the feelings it stirred up. "I was in the bathroom shaving and I looked at myself in the mirror," he says. "I thought, 'I don't like you very much. You're not being honest with the people you love, and most of all, you aren't being honest with yourself.'"

Accustomed to keeping such feelings deep inside, Randy didn't talk to his wife about the dream or the inner turmoil it created. But from that point on he started thinking about life in a different way, looking at the world from the perspective of a gay man trapped in a straight relationship. Though he knew it wasn't fair to his wife or children, Randy assumed his life would always be that way. Then, he met a man at the gym. It started as a friendship, but Randy quickly fell in love.

"I was still married, but once I met Tom it was like, 'This is where I should be,'" Randy says. "I met Tom in June. In December, my wife confronted me with the question of if I was gay. And I finally admitted it."

Looking back, Randy regrets that his ex-wife had to force him to tell the truth about his sexuality. "I regret that it had to be like that," he says. "I wish I could've been honest with her and everyone else from the get-go, but I wasn't and I didn't and that's the way it was."

Randy's ex felt angry and betrayed. Though she knew on an intellectual level that it wasn't her fault, that she hadn't done anything to "turn him gay," Randy believes she still felt ashamed.

"I did—I do still—love my ex-wife," Randy says, slowly. The pair are on speaking terms, but their relationship will always be strained. "It's just a different kind of love. At the time I finally came out, I told her, 'There is no other woman who could've gotten me to this point,' and I meant that. She has been instrumental in my life."

Though the intentions behind such statements like Randy's are good, hearing an ex-husband utter such words still stings, says Bonnie, a Pennsylvania woman whose husband came out to her as gay. This was many decades ago, and since then Bonnie has made it her life's mission to assist straight women who find out they are married to gay men.

"It's easy for me to say to a woman in this situation, 'It's not your fault,'" Bonnie says, but after years spent living with a man who's devoted so much of his life to "tricking himself into thinking he can live a straight life, many of these women have a hard time believing that if they had just somehow behaved differently they may have been able to keep their marriage together."

It's important for women with gay husbands to step back from their grief, anger, and shame and look at the problem from a different perspective. "Most gay men who married straight women didn't set out to trick their wives. They were actually trying to trick *themselves*. It's their problem. Not yours. They were fighting the odds," she says.

Bonnie says her marriage started out with a strong sexual connection, but after just a few months, her husband found ways to avoid intercourse. He accused her of being "oversexed" and "overaggressive." When the truth finally came out and they divorced, Bonnie had a hard time thinking of herself as a sexually attractive woman. It was like she shut down that side of herself.

"I became celibate for eleven years," she says. "It was the only reaction I could imagine for myself at the time."

Though celibacy helped her heal from the pain of her marriage, Bonnie doesn't think that's the solution for everyone. She advises women who are coming out of a relationship like hers to "give yourself the time you need to find out who you are again. Build up your self esteem and your sexual esteem. My heart breaks for women who were married to gay men for thirty, forty years. They've never had a straight man, never known what it is like to be with a man who actually desires them."

Later, Bonnie says, "I found a soul mate. I've been with him for almost twenty years now. Sex is an important part of our relationship. I am going to be sixty-two soon and sex is still good for me."

The truth must come out

In all but a very small number of cases, one partner's revelation that they are gay usually results in a breakup, Novell says. "In cases like this, a couple went into a relationship with one paradigm of sexuality. When one member announces that they actually prefer sexual relations with members of the same gender, the couple must then look at their alternatives, which can include integrating his or her gayness into the marriage. Achieving this would depend on the expansiveness of both partners' sexuality and their tolerance of infidelity."

Over the years, Novell has worked with a handful of couples who have agreed to stay together despite this revelation. Sometimes, he believes, the willingness to remain married despite one partner's homosexuality has to do with advancing age and waning sex drive.

"If a man or woman comes out in his or her sixties, it's quite a bit different than a man or woman coming out in his or her twenties," Novell says. "Have they had a sexless-but-loving marriage until this time? If so, the question to confront may be 'Can you integrate that new reality and expand your sexuality or, regardless of age, can you make an agreement that you are also allowed to have sex with other people?'" Though Novell's not sure he'd advise it, such marriages do exist, he insists. But both partners need to go into the arrangement honestly.

"In Hollywood," he says, with a quiet laugh, "women who choose this life are still called 'beards.'"

While sexuality may not be at the center of all partnered relationships, honesty should be. Lewis's work as a couples therapist is also focused on the larger network of family and friends that orbit around her clients. Honesty is central to keeping that network strong, Lewis says, and in all but a very small number of cases, it is extremely difficult to be honest about a change in professed sexual orientation while remaining in a partnership.

In many of those cases, Lewis says, "I can't help save a marriage but I can help heal a relationship. When a partner acknowledges 'I'm gay or lesbian and I've decided I need to be honest with myself and go live that life,' what I've been able to do in most of those families is help the newly owned gay partner stay connected to the family and help the other partner grieve and deal with the anger. Then they can figure out how to go about readjusting their lives."

After he came out to his wife and moved out of their home, Randy still didn't tell their children that he was gay. His family warned him against it, saying that the knowledge would be confusing and emotionally damaging for the kids, then still pre-teens. They didn't need to think about their father as a sexual being. Now he regrets that he waited so long.

"I wish I could do it over," Randy says. Then, his ex did the outing for him. One day, in a fit of frustration, she told the kids that their father was gay. For a time, the children were angry at Randy, but not for the reasons he'd feared.

"They weren't pissed that I was gay," he says, shaking his head and chuckling. "They were pissed that I didn't tell them myself."

For a long time, Randy felt guilty about not being open with his kids. Later, he sat down with them and made a vow. "I said," he says, "'I was completely and totally wrong to keep this from you. I should've never agreed to not tell you the truth and I will never, ever do that again.'"

Randy says that knowing the truth about their father helped his children survive the divorce. Finally understanding why their dad had seemed to feel angry and trapped for so many years helped them navigate their own lives.

"At one point after I came out, my son told me, 'You know, you weren't the easiest person to live with for the last couple of years,'" Randy says. "He said I'd blow up at the smallest things. I wasn't aware that I was doing that at the time. My son said, 'Sometimes we'd just walk around on eggshells around you because we didn't know what mood you'd be in.' Once I came out to everyone, my personality just evened out."

Ever since, Randy's been committed to living an honest life. When his partner died of cancer after seven years together, both of their families came to the funeral. The split still causes some pain, but Randy believes that everyone can breathe easier now.

"That's what I want for me and my loved ones," Randy says. "After all these years of being dishonest, telling the truth feels so good."

Friendly fire

From Melissa Seligman's point of view, David never seemed like a soldier. When she met the man who would one day become her husband, she recalls that he was a "real granola head, an environmental-science major." And that's what attracted her to him.

But David was also in the Army reserves, and, Seligman adds, he possessed "a strong sense of service." Still, she figured that once David's reserve duty was over, he'd be done with military life. He thought so, too. Not long after graduating from college, the pair married and moved to Montana, where David enrolled in graduate school and Seligman set out to find a teaching job. "We were going to live in the mountains and hug trees," she says, only half-jokingly.

Seligman never set out to marry a military man. "My father was a Vietnam vet, and I grew up in a home that was full of PTSD," she says. "Having lived with that for so long made me leery of all things military. All I knew about military service was 'You go to war and you come home and feel alienated and alone.'"

Then, a few days after the September 11 terrorist attacks, David told Melissa he wanted to sign up for active duty. As a U.S. citizen, he felt it was his obligation to serve his country, Seligman says. As David's wife, Melissa couldn't help feeling afraid and abandoned.

"I knew that this was what he felt he needed to do," Seligman says. "But that didn't really make it any easier for me. I felt like I'd married one kind of man and then, without much warning, he changed into someone else."

And on top of that, anther major life shift occurred. "About a week after my husband signed up for active duty, I found out I was pregnant," Seligman recalls. David would be shipping out for Afghanistan in a matter of weeks. "Basically, we spent that whole pregnancy apart."

The couple was stationed at Fort Drum, in northern New York State. While David was overseas, Melissa felt lost and stuck. She couldn't find a job. She worried about becoming a mother. She had a hard time making friends on base. And after her first child was born, Seligman struggled with postpartum depression.

"I became a mother in an isolated place that I had not picked," she tells me. Because she didn't want to distract or worry her husband while he was deployed, Seligman tried not to talk about her problems when they spoke. David had an important job to do. "I didn't want to rattle him. I did not want to make him lose focus on his job. That wouldn't be safe. I could not fully understand the wide range of emotions he was going through during a deployment, but I tried to be sympathetic. When he finally came home, I was all over the place."

David's first deployment was followed by another, and their first child by a second. Because her husband spent so much time in another part of the world, Seligman was a single parent.

While she appreciated that technology allowed her to speak with her husband while he was deployed overseas, she began to realize that the pressure of communicating her true feelings across thousands of miles wore on her. She began to dread their conversations and the stress they created for her and her children. So she came up with a solution: She'd write her husband long letters—essentially expansions of her personal journal entries—and he'd write back. Then they'd mail their letters the old-fashioned way. David loved the idea.

"Communicating this way was a real godsend for our marriage," Seligman says. "It forced us to slow down and really think about what we were saying to one another. It gave us something to look forward to."

Seligman was so enthusiastic about the success of this new/old mode of communication that she wrote an essay, titled "One Husband, Two Kids, Three Deployments." In May 2009, it was published in the *New York Times*. Her essay reads, in part:

> Writing allowed us to regain control of our marriage. On paper, our memories came to life. Through letters we could share our concerns without worrying that we'd be misinterpreted.

> As I read David's words, I smelled his cologne, I heard him whistle while I cooked, I felt his hand on the small of my back. Amelia would stuff her daddy's letters into her pockets and take them with her to the playground. At night, she would beg me to read the letters again. Over and over until she felt content enough to sleep.

> We poured our hearts into the letters, and there were no time delays in the way, no fears that an argument would be unfinished when the satellite dropped.

> I know I'm not the first military spouse who has struggled to communicate with a loved one on deployment—and I know I won't be the last. For those who came before me, the burden to overcome was communicating without technology—waiting months for letters to arrive. For me and those still to come, it's learning to communicate despite technology."

Not all technology is bad, however. A few years ago, Seligman discovered the amazing power of social media when she teamed up with Christina Piper, a veteran and fellow military spouse, to create *Her War Her Voice*, a website that offers connections and support for women who serve in the military or are partnered with service members. The project began during one of David's long deployment, and almost immediately after the first post went live, it took off.

"All of these women started coming out of the woodwork," Seligman says. It was heartening to see that there were so many women like her out there, people who had the same fears, concerns, and struggles. "Now we have a strong community of 8,000 spouses from around the branches talking about issues like PTSD, postpartum depression, coming out of deployment. It's a community of women coming together and writing about these things. Together, we've built this amazing resource that makes us all stronger."

Husband vs. hero

Because Seligman's father was a veteran who struggled with PTSD, she knew that it was nearly impossible to return from a war without some lasting emotional trauma. As her husband cycled in and out of multiple deployments, Seligman watched him closely. After David came home from his third deployment, they both noticed that something was off.

"David went from being outgoing and kind to depressed and repressed and paranoid," she recalls. "In many ways, he became like the father I grew up with." Seligman was dismayed but wasn't surprised. "He'd gone through three deployments. He'd seen some horrible things."

To help David cope with the aftereffects of his military service, the couple sought counseling, individually and as a couple. The counseling, which, for David, included eye movement desensitization and reprocessing (EMDR), a nontraditional type of psychotherapy that has shown to have great success in treating patients with PTSD, has been essential in helping them rediscover the strengths they possessed before they were separated by war.

Interestingly, Seligman's father experienced a flare of his own PTSD symptoms after David went to war. He, too, sought counseling for his condition, and is learning to cope with memories of his own wartime experiences.

For now, Seligman says her husband's PTSD has "somewhat subsided." She wants to make the point that there is a misconception that PTSD is a diagnosis that plagues someone for a very long time. "It can," she says, "but there is also the possibility of healing and acceptance. That's the point I'm currently seeing my husband and father at."

Understanding the unique struggle of veterans is important, Seligman insists, but part of the healing process is also remembering that somewhere deep inside of that veteran is the man she fell in love with.

"There's a very distinct difference between what it takes to love a husband and be proud of a hero," Seligman says. She works to reconcile—and appreciate—those two sides while re-creating a healthy, whole person.

Seligman sees choosing to face the aftereffects of wartime trauma head-on as taking a brave step. People who suffer from PTSD get a bad rap in the media, she says. But many who struggle with the disorder manage to live normal, productive lives.

"From the outside, people see someone with PTSD as someone who is really suffering," Seligman says. "The truth is their humanity has been hurt. But choosing to work on healing, choosing not to hurt yourself or others is taking a heroic path. There are countless people in the military who are affected by PTSD and still function beautifully every day. They are choosing to keep moving forward. I don't know if I could do that if I saw the death and destruction that my husband and father did."

Beyond counseling, Seligman says David helps bring himself back to his pre-service self through his focus on hobbies like working on his car and brewing beer. "He has found ways to tap into who he is as a person," she says. She focuses on her own mental health through her website, her writing ("I'm working on a novel," she tells me) and progressing toward her black belt in Taekwondo.

These days, the Seligman family lives in Columbia, South Carolina, where David, who still has another decade of service remaining, is stationed at Fort Jackson. For now, he's working stateside as a recruiter, but they both know that he will soon be redeployed. Until then, the couple chooses to focus on the present, by spending time alone and as a family, immersing themselves in everyday activities that help shut out the noise of the world and bring them back to the basic elements of who they've been—and who they want to be.

"For my husband, one of the quickest ways to reconnect is to go camping," Seligman says. "Then he can smell all those outdoor smells and he and I can sit in front of a campfire for hours and not speak. When we do that, I feel connected to him very quickly. Despite the war and all of our separations, that part of David is still very much alive. That side is still very much thriving." That's the kind of reassurance Seligman needs.

Change-survival tips from partners who've been there:

+ **Reach out to friends and family,** says Bonnie. After she and her husband split up, she was left to care for their children alone. "After our divorce," she says, "the first thing I had to do was rally support for myself. My family and friends stood by me as a single mother. I didn't have many financial resources at the beginning, so it was important for me to put together a system of people who could support me."

+ **Understand the importance of healing for soldiers coming home from war,** Melissa Seligman advises. "It was my husband who said, 'Everybody has a right to their own 100 percent.' For us, we set out to get help one day when we were both sitting together and he said, 'I can't keep going on like this.' He sought counseling, once he realized I didn't see him as a monster but as a normal human being who was experiencing pain."

+ This can be tough, but Carol says she **tried not to feel sorry for herself** when her life partner became severely disabled. "I decided I wouldn't feel like I'd been cheated. Bill was my family, and that's what I wanted to do for him."

+ Enough lies, Randy says. **Even though it can be hard, tell the truth.** In the end, it will make important relationships stronger. "After I finally told my children the truth about being gay, a whole new level of our relationship opened up," he says. "When they realized I was being honest with them, they started being open and honest with me."

+ **Speak up.** Explain your situation. It helps build connections and increase understanding, Lynette says. "I always tell people about the stroke, especially teachers and new people. I explain that it is such a fundamental part of our family. They'd have to know that to understand what is going on at home. It humanizes us. It's not the first thing I tell people, but it is a pretty big part of our lives."

Chapter 5

How to Survive Unemployment

Losing a job is a one-two punch. First, there's the moment you actually get laid off or fired—and the accompanying stressful days leading up to that event, where you can sense that things are falling apart at work and there's nothing you can do to fix it. That should be the knockout punch—but it's not.

Like a scrappy, prideful prizefighter outsized by your opponent, you reel from a direct blow to the head (the layoff, the firing, the order to pack up your stuff and leave), but you shake it off, stand upright, and walk out the door with your head held high and your knees wobbly. The final blow comes a day or so later, when you wake up and realize that you don't know where your next paycheck is coming from. Bam: KO punch.

You're out cold, until someone—or something—pours a bucket of cold water over your head. Then you're back at it.

Lee Ann Taylor, a spunky, sassy radio DJ from New York state, took her first punch one Monday morning in 2007. She'd been working as a program director at a country-music station. She knew finances were shaky at the station, but she had no idea that her neck was on the block: She'd just taken a group of listeners on a promotional weekend trip to Los Angeles, and from her perspective her job felt secure.

"I got back from the trip on Monday," Taylor tells me, "and bam. I was out of there. Told to pack up my stuff in boxes and leave. I should've seen the signs, but for some reason I was totally blindsided."

On the day of her layoff, Taylor, forty-five, managed to pack up and leave calmly, but on Tuesday morning she woke up angry.

"I was ticked off," she says. "I was pissed. I felt like the reason

I lost my job was because the station owner was spending irresponsibly. It didn't feel fair that I had to pay for his mismanagement. I felt that way for two days. First, I went through the boxes of stuff I brought home from work and threw stuff out. Then I still had all this excess energy so I started tearing through my house, purging all the junk. On day three, the anger faded, and I started feeling worried, like, 'What the hell am I going to do?' I was shell-shocked."

That night, Taylor regrouped. "By day four, I had pulled a game plan together."

It turns out, that plan included flying to a country-music conference in Nashville. She'd been scheduled to go for her job, but when that fell apart, she decided to pay for her own ticket. It was a good move. At the conference, Taylor was able to renew industry connections and make new contacts. She gathered leads that eventually turned into two part-time DJ jobs. Things, it seemed, were already looking up for Taylor.

But Taylor's journey in the mossy jungle of unemployment was only beginning.

I've spent time in that same dark jungle myself. Over a decade ago, I was working as an editor at a national magazine when I got the heave-ho. Job insecurity is the name of the game in the magazine business—a former boss (the third I worked under at the magazine in five years) even told me, "You haven't made it until you've been fired"—but those kind words didn't make it feel any better when I realized that I was on my way out. Still, when I was given my final marching orders, I packed up my things and left, like Lee Ann, with my head held as high as I could hold it. But it still was a blow.

After so many years spent relying on an employer for intellectual stimulation, social interaction, and financial stability, suddenly being without a job was unnerving. I felt a bit like a dinghy adrift at sea.

At sea

Taylor knows that feeling all too well. While she quickly rebounded from her 2007 layoff by landing those two part-time gigs, it didn't take long to realize that the economy was collapsing. Crippled by shrinking ad revenues, radio stations around the country were cutting staff. Taylor realized she'd been lucky to have found two part-time jobs. The way things were going in her industry, she knew that it would be next to impossible to find another steady full-time gig.

"I lost my job right before 10,000 people got laid off in radio," Taylor says. "There were absolutely no on-air jobs."

Taylor's two part-time DJ slots were at stations more than an hour away from her home, and with gas running four dollars a gallon, a long commute for less than twenty hours of work a week didn't make financial sense. Even with two jobs, Taylor's income was low enough for her to qualify for unemployment checks. So when she was laid off from one of the jobs, it actually felt like a relief. She gave her notice at the other station and decided to redouble her efforts looking for a full-time position.

"I've worked a lot of different jobs in my life," Taylor says, ticking off an impressive list of former positions that includes pharmacy technician, nanny, personal assistant, and paralegal, "but deep down I've always thought of myself as a radio person." So when radio jobs dried up, Taylor felt lost. She knew she'd have to diversify her search if she wanted to find a job, and she did, creating several different versions of her résumé that highlighted different areas of expertise.

But still nothing came through.

"I sent out at least 800 résumés and I got not one reply," Taylor tells me. "Back in the day, when you applied for a job, at least you'd get a form letter if they weren't interested in hiring you. But now, when there are so many job seekers out there, employers feel like they can just ignore you. They act like you never existed."

Karyn Frisch is a career counselor at Quincy Career Center in Quincy, Massachusetts. These days, as the economy shifts, she increasingly thinks of herself as a "reinvention coordinator," helping her clients look back at their work history and identify new job categories they may be interested in pursuing.

"You lose your identity when you lose your job," Frisch says, adding that for people like Taylor who strongly identify with a struggling industry, there is always the added stress that your livelihood is going away. "Increasingly, some of the jobs that my clients have lost are not coming back," Frisch says, "and in those cases I'm working with people who have to completely reinvent themselves. This is a big process, and it takes time and emotional strength."

Frisch has seen too many of her clients crack under the stress of long-term unemployment. A child of working-class parents, she left a higher-paying job at a recruiting firm to take her post at the Quincy Career Center. It seemed like the right place for her.

Frisch has an almost evangelical approach to her work. "Before coming here, I worked at three different recruiting firms," she says. "The money was fine, but I didn't really care about the job. I like helping people find work, but the people I'd contact for the recruiting firms usually already had a job. It wasn't as rewarding as helping someone who really needs to work find a job. In this job, I feel like I'm giving back."

Turning point

There were times when Taylor felt like it took all of her emotional strength just to keep applying for jobs. Some days, it felt like her life was falling apart. Her marriage broke up and she couldn't afford the rent on her apartment, so she packed up her stuff and moved home to live closer to family. At this point, she'd been unemployed for over a year.

Back at home, sending out résumés without any response, Taylor felt like she was living under a cloud.

"I got very depressed," Taylor tells me. "I was at loose ends. I felt like nothing was ever going to work out for me again. Eventually, I decided to hospitalize myself for the weekend to get myself together."

Taylor sees her hospitalization as a turning point. "I checked myself in because I wanted a break," she says. "While I was in there, I learned quite a bit about other people. There were people there who were so talented but thought that they were worthless. There was this sixteen-year-old girl with an amazing singing voice who just couldn't imagine going on living. I got this feeling of 'There but for the grace of God go I.' I said to myself, 'Enough of the pity party! Let's get cracking again.' This was a low point in my journey. My energy was all gone. But when I got out, I picked right up where I left off. I got really serious. I was energized."

Taylor used her new energy to take on the job search in a more creative, aggressive way. Experience had taught her that she was getting nowhere sending out endless copies of her résumé and applying for jobs, so she decided to go after work from a new perspective. She identified her dream jobs and researched the people who worked at those companies. She began crafting laser-targeted cover letters and résumés and sending them to specific employers. Then she picked up the phone and tried calling people at those companies just to introduce herself.

Taylor's revamped approach to job hunting is exactly the tactic that Amy Lindgren, a syndicated jobs columnist and career counselor, suggests to her clients. In her popular employment workshops, Lindgren advises turning the traditional job search on its ear.

"The thrust of my workshops is that you need to do a job search from the inside out—rather than the outside in," Lindgren says. "Heading in, you determine what kind of salary you require, what sort of responsibilities you seek. Then you identify the job that would meet those goals. After that, you go and find that job, and identify the people you need to connect with to get it."

Taylor also spent time researching ways to draw attention to herself as a job seeker. She saw that CNN had a feature called "The 30-Second Pitch," where job seekers were invited to come on air and talk about their skills for 30 seconds. With an "I have nothing to lose," attitude, Taylor sent a tweet to CNN anchor Kyra Phillips. She explained her situation, and told Phillips that she'd like to be on "The 30-Second Pitch."

"Kyra responded to me," Taylor says, laughing. "She said, 'E-mail me your pitch.' So I did, and they selected me to be on the show in November 2009."

After Taylor appeared on CNN, things started happening fast. She got a call from a radio station in Binghamton, New York. They were looking for a co-host for their drive-time show, and they thought Taylor could be a good match. "They were intrigued," Taylor says. "They thought my appearance on the show showed that I have a good work ethic and I'm really willing to put myself out there to get what I want."

Three years later, Taylor is still morning co-host (with Big Wally) at The Whale 99.1 FM.

"I love this job," she says. "It's comfortable. Six months after I moved here, I found my current husband through the radio station. I had to sing with the band that won our contest and he was the lead singer. Good things happen if you just say, 'What's the worst that can happen?' You have to be willing to put yourself out there, to not be afraid of making a fool of yourself."

Falling into the gap

Like Taylor, many workers have recently seen their industries contract. Take Shannon. As 2008 neared, she was a successful vice president at a major Wall Street investment bank. The thirty-five-year-old had made a name for herself as one of a few young women in her industry. She was pulling in the big bucks, working long hours, and enjoying the single life in New York. She felt like she lived a charmed life.

"I'm the type of person who's been successful my whole life," Shannon tells me, candidly. "I was smart in school and I did well. I was always toward the top of my class. It wasn't that everything came easy for me, but I'm a hard worker and it paid off."

In 2007, most workers weren't aware that a Great Recession was about to hit, but employees in Shannon's working group knew that something was up. Part of her job was to make loans for buildings. When the housing crisis hit and the subprime disaster came to light, Shannon's industry went down.

"The financial crisis hit us first," she says with a low laugh, the earlier bravado faded from her voice. "As early as July 2007, I knew that something was going to happen to my job. For almost six months, we'd just sit around at work. We went from working 24/7 to nothing. As of August 1, business totally shut down. And it never came back. For all that time, they were creating busy work for us. It was a joke."

Shannon was watching TV when she learned that she was probably going to lose her job.

"I knew it was happening because CNBC announced it the day before. So I packed up my stuff and waited for the official announcement." It didn't take long. When Shannon went into work the next day, the layoffs began, just like CNBC said they would.

"It was just a matter of waiting around the office until they came in to lay us off," Shannon says. "When they did, they went and got my boss first. Then they got me after. Because I was ready for it, I was pretty calm when it was happening."

There were about a hundred people employed in Shannon's group. Twenty-five of them were laid off that day, along with thousands of others throughout the company.

In a matter of weeks, New York's Financial District turned into a ghost town. Shannon told me she began looking for work almost immediately after she walked out of her office, but there was nothing.

"I couldn't get another job in my industry," she says. "There was nothing else." It was like living in a company town after the company closed. You could almost see the tumbleweeds rolling down the street.

The stress of watching the working world she loved crumble was immense, says Shannon. She felt exhausted and depressed and didn't know where to turn. When her parents offered to put her up at their Florida condo for the month, she jumped at the chance.

"It was the best thing I did," Shannon says now. "Being in New York in the winter with no work and nothing to do is depressing. I realized I could do everything I needed to do from Florida. I made a few phone calls, sent out a few résumés, sat on the beach. It was good for my psyche."

It's not unusual for laid-off workers to experience depression and other stress-related health problems, says Lindgren.

"There are studies now that have found that when people get laid off they are more susceptible to a range of health concerns, like upper-respiratory infections, colds, bronchitis," she says. "There is also an uptick in the onset of type 2 diabetes."

Kate Strully, professor of sociology at the State University of New York at Albany, published a paper in 2009 that found that after an employer is shut down, workers have an 83 percent higher chance of experiencing stress-related health problems. Beyond diabetes, those problems include arthritis, high blood pressure, and psychiatric issues. And job loss also often puts a strain on personal relationships, causing friendships to fade, families to feud, and marriages to falter. While Shannon's entire company did not go out of business, much of her industry did, and the impact on those who were laid off and looking for work was severe. People got sick, business and professional relationships struggled, and the national economy teetered.

"One thing to keep in mind is that oftentimes these physical and emotional stressors tend to go hand in hand," Strully says. "Layoffs, for instance, tend to put stress on marriages and increase the odds of divorce. Divorce increases the odds of chronic illness. These things tend to be highly intertwined."

Career casualty

The same economy that exterminated Shannon's job prospects also sent Norm Elrod's career into a tailspin. A New York-based marketing and communications professional, he has been laid off four times in the last eight years, in 2000, 2006, 2007, and 2008.

Norm's first layoff was at the height of the dot-com bust. He was working for an Internet start-up, and when the investment money dried up, the company went belly-up.

"The first time I was laid off, the whole company shut down," Elrod, forty, recalls. Somehow, knowing that everyone he worked with was in the same boat felt oddly comforting. Subsequent layoffs, when only a select few employees were let go, were more painful. "The second, third, and fourth times I was laid off, the company went on without me. That's a real blow to your confidence. It's hard to imagine that life can go on without you, you know? As much as they tell you your layoff is not performance-based, you're still being rejected and others aren't."

After Elrod's first layoff, there were still jobs available and he was able to find another position in a few months. Same goes for the next couple of layoffs. But as the US economy continued to fail, with entire sectors like Shannon's drying up, Elrod's jobs got less and less dependable. By 2008, out of work again with thousands of other New Yorkers pounding the pavement, Norm decided that he needed to develop a skill that would set him apart from the competition. And the truth was, he admitted to me, he also needed something do keep himself occupied during the long work-less days. He was out of work that time for a year and a half.

"Nobody was hiring anybody back then," Norm says. "Absolutely nothing was happening." Like Taylor, he decided he needed to develop a skill that set him apart from the competition. "I started thinking that I need another way to distinguish myself, to improve myself, to get myself out there. I got the idea to launch a website about the experience of being unemployed in America."

To launch his site—joblessandless.com—Norm had to teach himself basic website design and administration skills.

"There was a bit of a learning curve," he says with a snort. "I didn't know anything about running a website, but I knew I needed to learn those skills." In the end, it was a good gamble. Elrod was able to add the valuable phrase "website design and administration" to his résumé, and resourceful optimization led members of the national media to his site.

"When I set up my blog, unemployment was spiking and there was a lot of news about unemployed people." Elrod says. "It was a big story. I knew one way to get decent searches was to give your site a name that included a word that people were searching for. That's how my site got its name." In the end, Norm and his site were mentioned in the *New York Times* and the *Wall Street Journal*. He was also interviewed by Katie Couric on *The Today Show*. The attention led to several freelance jobs, and ultimately to the job Elrod has today, as a project manager at a major media company.

Being tossed around from so many jobs has given Norm a different perspective on work. While his parents both had steady, traditional jobs—as a public-school teacher and a federal government worker—he knows better than to believe that the job he holds today will be the same job he holds in ten years.

"I've been laid off four times," Elrod says. "How much loyalty can I have to one workplace? I know that as soon as budgets get cut or the economy goes in a different direction, I'm just a number on a piece of paper. I don't have a job for life."

Elrod believes he can be a good worker—without buying the company line. Even though he has been at his current job for a couple of years now, Elrod still resists the classic trappings of employee commitment, the "I'm here for good," tchotchkes that people use to adorn their workspaces.

"There is nothing up in my cube," he chuckles. "I have the office phone list and I have a list of other things related to work and I have branch contacts, but I don't really have any personal items up on my desk at all. Not a picture. I don't know if it is conscious or unconscious. I have empty drawers in my desk. I don't have stuff to put in them. All I have in my cube is a tube of lotion and a sweatshirt. But I still work hard. I still contribute as much as anyone. I just keep work in perspective."

In a perverse way, Elrod believes that the instability in his work life has given him a sense of inner calm.

"Eight months ago they reorganized my department," he tells me. "Nobody lost their job, but for many people it was unsettling. They were just putting people in different areas and refocusing things. My younger co-workers were distraught, but I was just like, 'Tell me where you want me to go next.' I didn't miss a beat. I knew what it was like. I'd been there so many times before."

Identity crisis

Since Elrod's career path has been rutted almost from the start, he has no expectation that he will ever land the mythical "job for life" that would last him into a comfortable retirement. But there still is a generation of workers—closer to Elrod's parents' age—that grew up with the idea that if they worked hard enough, they could someday find a steady job with a pension.

Rusty, a kind, soft-spoken sixty-three-year-old, whose subtle drawl reveals his rural Missouri birthplace, is part of that generation.

As his nickname suggests, Rusty's got a neat, short-trimmed

head of light-red hair. The son of an agricultural engineer, Rusty planned to follow in his father's footsteps. He earned a bachelor's and a master's degree in agricultural engineering, and after graduating in the early 1970s, landed his first engineering job at the multinational agricultural equipment manufacturer John Deere.

"It was my dream job," Rusty says. "When I graduated, I interviewed with three different agricultural companies and Deere was the one I selected. It was just where I wanted to be. At the time, I figured I'd be there for life."

With a generous pension plan and strong benefits, John Deere employs many workers who have been with the company for decades. Rusty was set up for that sort of career path. His creative mind was fueled by the design side of his job, but after a decade at work he began to feel frustrated when he noticed that he was doing less designing and more managing. Nearly fifteen years in, Rusty decided to make the leap to a start-up company that promised more design opportunities.

"I was the typical graduate from engineering school," Rusty explained to me. "I thought, 'I'm going to design farm equipment.' Then by the time I was thirty years old, I was no longer designing anything. I was still heavily engaged in engineering work but I haven't designed anything for years. The work world had changed drastically from when I started out. This other job promised that I would be able to do more of what I loved to do."

Rusty's leap away from the stability of John Deere unwittingly led him into a new world economy, where workers are expendable and company loyalty reaps few rewards. After Rusty had been at the start-up just one year, the company did not renew his contract. Out of a job for the first time in his life, Rusty embarked on what would eventually become a fifteen-year odyssey, where he moved from job to job, forced to part ways with several employers because of cutbacks, shutdowns, and economic shifts.

"My first period of unemployment lasted for six months," Rusty says. "It felt dramatic to me at the time, because I'd grown up with a dad who always had a good, reliable job, and here I was out on my ear due to poor judgment on my part. I'd left a good, steady job for something much less reliable. It was somewhat an admission of failure on my part." Rusty had always defined his identity by his work. It was how he introduced himself, what he did during the day. Being unstable at work made him feel unstable inside. At one point during that period, Rusty was unemployed for a year and a half.

Without a job title, Rusty was unsure how to define himself to others.

"I wasn't associated with a business, and for a man my age, that's an identity loss," he says. "Think about how you usually introduce yourself. Before I lost my job, I was a VP and a project manager. When I was unemployed, I had no way to describe who I was." He pauses for a minute and then adds, softly, "I don't know if I ever came up with a way to handle it."

In her more than two decades of counseling job seekers, Lindgren has seen that layoffs are especially hard on professional, white-collar men.

"I've seen that higher-level men are often unprepared mentally for layoffs," she says. "A lot of these guys think that they got their job because they deserved to be there. They never even seemed to recognize that they'd probably had at least an invisible helping hand in the first place. When a guy in this position loses a job, it seems like the whole world was turned upside down. And you can't blame them. Their sense of identity was all wrapped up in their work. This phenomenon was especially true when I started out in this work."

In the mid-1980s, Lindgren remembers a client who was so ashamed of losing his executive position that he resorted to an elaborate deception.

"Turns out, he didn't tell his wife that he had been laid off," she says. "He'd been dressing up in his suit in the morning, grabbing his briefcase and going to the library. He came to see me for career counseling, and of course he didn't tell me this was what he was doing. So one day I had a question for him. I called his house during the day and asked for him. His wife said he wasn't home, he was at work. I asked, 'Did he get a job?' The jig was up."

Nadya Fouad, distinguished professor of educational psychology at the University of Wisconsin–Milwaukee, says that when you think about the American core belief in the importance of work as a source of self-definition, it's not that surprising that high-earning men who lose their jobs would struggle to redefine their place in the world.

"Think about the identity that's wrapped up in your work in this country," Fouad says. "This is particularly true for men. When you lose your job, you've lost who you are, and when you can't get hired, it feels like a personal rejection. Even though we talk about the importance of keeping work separate from the rest of our life, the two definitely intermingle, and the stress of being without that main defining element can be overwhelming."

Still, with all the attention paid to mass layoffs nationwide, there appears to be less shame associated with job loss, even for white-collar workers.

"These days, as a culture, we've come to absorb the idea that layoffs are rotten, but it's not a shameful thing to lose your job," Lindgren says. "My clients now realize that this kind of thing happens to everyone. They all know somebody who's been through it. There is still anxiety but less shame."

Over his years of bouncing from job to job, Rusty felt like he was under a deadline of sorts. As he got older, he feared that potential employers would pass him by, either because they thought he was overqualified for the work, or simply because they'd rather hire a younger worker.

Most employers wouldn't come out and say that, Rusty says, but he saw that "at forty-five, it really was difficult to find a job, especially when you hit the one-year mark of unemployment. At that point, it starts getting pretty rough."

While Rusty's wife had a job, her income wasn't enough for the two of them to live on forever. When Rusty was out of work, there were times when the pair had to borrow from a life insurance policy just to keep up the premiums. They used up all of their savings, didn't contribute to retirement accounts, and went without medical insurance.

"There were times when if one of us had broken a bone, we didn't know how we'd pay for it," Rusty says.

Keep on moving

Even though he really needed the money, Rusty felt that it was unrealistic—and unhealthy—to devote himself full time to a job search. So he decided to ramp up one of his hobbies. He'd been interested in showroom stock car racing for years, and he became more involved in that world, going to events, getting to know drivers, and eventually joining a pit crew.

"I didn't want to become a couch potato," Rusty says. "The racing world is a good match for a guy like me." His engineering background means he knows his way around an engine. And he's quickly come to realize that the connections and friendships he made there extended beyond the racetrack.

"The friends I made through racing are some of the best people I've known in my lifetime," he says. He looks back on that period of his life fondly, as a time of self-exploration and expansion.

It was not, however, a time of making money. Looking back, Rusty wonders if he should've found a part-time job to help pay the bills while he was looking for work. At the time, though, he felt like taking a job as a cashier at Target or in an auto-parts store would have been a soul-crushing distraction.

"At the end, it was a little tricky for us financially. If you were to ask, 'What's one of the lingering effects of that period of unemployment?' I'd have to say that the biggest thing is that I'll need to work another three or four years to get to a period when I can retire comfortably. I lost the ability to save for our future during the time I wasn't working."

During that period, Rusty worked hard to keep up his professional contacts, attending industry conferences on his own and keeping in touch with former colleagues. He landed other engineering jobs, but they never lasted long. Then, in 2000, he heard about another job at John Deere. He landed it and happily made his way back into the fold.

Rusty tells me he's delighted that he finally made it back to his former employer, though as a sixty-three-year-old engineer, he stands out among his peers. The company is known for long-term employees who start right out of college and stay until retirement. Most engineers his age are already living on their pensions—or are close to retirement.

Rusty spells it out like this. "Most people my age at Deere, they've put in the time and they're gone. They don't work until they are sixty-five. They take the pension and go. Now, if I walk into a meeting, I'm the senior citizen," he laughs. "I feel like I am older than everybody else here, but at the same time I don't feel like I'm outdated. I think my life experience is helpful in many situations."

While it would be good to retire right now, Rusty says that mixed with regret over his "journey in the employment wilderness" is a sense of pride in living through difficult times. He has a hard-won perspective that helps him see that employers do not always deserve our unending loyalty.

"Most of the people my age still left at Deere are thirty-five-plus-year employees," Rusty says. "Their attitude is 'Deere owes me and I owe them. We're together forever.' Let's just say I appreciate everything that the company provides for me, but I'm also skeptical sometimes. I see the difference between a job and a family. I know which one is more important. I'm not counting the years to retirement. My goal is to work, get the most out my work—and do a good job."

DIY

Maybe the best jobs are the ones we invent for ourselves.

A decade ago, Bob, a fifty-year-old advertising executive, got the boot from his agency job. That layoff took him by surprise, but after many years in the ad industry he knew that when clients fade away, agencies often do some personnel trimming to keep budgets in line. He figured he'd just ask around at other firms and line up a spot right away, but after calling and e-mailing most of his contacts, nothing materialized. "The market was tight at the time," Bob says, adding that other traditional ways of finding work—posting a résumé on websites like CareerBuilder or Monster and going on informational interviews—wasn't panning out.

"After spending two months looking around," he says, "I quickly figured out that the money was going to run dry. My wife doesn't work outside of the home, so I am the sole breadwinner in our family. I had a lot of pressure on me to earn a salary."

This was when Bob decided he had to put his years of advertising experience to work. He needed to create an ad campaign for himself. Since his layoff, he'd done a bit of contract work for some contacts—various small jobs that paid a couple hundred dollars a pop—so he was confident that he was flexible enough to do a range of work for any type of client.

"I prepared a little sales collateral about the services I could offer," Bob says. Then he took a leap of faith. "One morning, I drove to an office park near my house. I didn't take a résumé, just my flier. Then"—he pauses for breath to demonstrate the way he gathered his courage—"I just started knocking on doors. I went door to door through that office park, cold-calling businesses."

It was a long day.

"In some of the businesses," Bob says, "I'd walk in and they treat me like a person selling a copier or a roll of toilet paper. They'd look at me like 'What the hell do you want?' Sometimes I'd encounter a receptionist who was polite and cordial, but they did a good job of screening, of keeping me away from the person I really needed to talk to. But most people I encountered would listen when I told them what I was up to. Then they'd politely say, 'We don't have a need for something like that.'"

But Bob's DIY job-hunt technique paid off.

"Late that afternoon, I ended up at a place very close to my house," he says, clearly still surprised by his luck. "It was a $10 million start-up company with a good, viable product." With his "sales brain" turned on, Bob struck up a conversation with the receptionist.

"I connected with her somehow and listened to what she was telling me about the company and their needs. On the spot, I tuned my pitch to match what she was talking about. She finally said, 'We are thinking about hiring a marketing person. Here's who you should talk to about the job.' I bugged this guy for several weeks, calling, leaving messages, and sending e-mails. Finally one day he called me up out of the blue and said, 'Let's meet for breakfast.' I ended up getting a forty-hour-a-week contract with them. I did that for about 18 months."

That long-term contract ultimately led to a full-time communications job at another company, but Bob still fondly remembers his time as an independent business owner. It was a tense time to be sure, not knowing where his next paycheck was coming from, but it was also an invigorating and freeing time. Bob realized that he was the master of his own destiny.

Not everyone is suited for self-employment, Lindgren acknowledges, but those who are can reap serious rewards. While she doesn't think all workers should go into business for themselves, she does hope that her clients will at least look beyond limited definitions of what careers they can aspire to. Like Bob, Lindgren believes that a good portion of the job-search process is choosing the career you want and developing a sales pitch for yourself.

"People put themselves in boxes," Lindgren says. "But limiting yourself only limits your options. It is your career and your life. You get to choose what happens. Ask yourself, 'Am I choosing my future, or am I just tumbling down a path?' If you're not intentional, not choosing your next step, you are making your history into your destiny."

At first, when Bob was laid off and couldn't quickly find a replacement job, he felt discouraged. He saw that for every worker that was let go, there were many other similar workers waiting in line to fill their place. But when he decided to set out on his own and create work for himself, he achieved a sense of freedom and self-confidence.

"I have to remember that at work, at least, I'm actually not that unique," he says. "There are a thousand people out there who could do what I am doing. Realizing this helped me to put it all in perspective. I understand that the most important place for me is at home with my family and friends, the place where I'm most irreplaceable."

Learning from the long haul

Frisch says that in her experience, it's not uncommon for a person to be out of work for as long as seven months to a year. And in tough economic times, workers in specific sectors can go without work for even longer.

That was definitely the case for Shannon. Remember how her industry all but faded into thin air in response to the 2008 economic collapse? For months after her layoff, after she returned from her time with her parents in Florida, Shannon felt like she was living in an echo chamber.

"I'd make calls," she recalls. "No one would return them. I'd send out résumés. Nothing. Everything in New York had dried up."

As the months stretched out and no job appeared to be on the horizon, Shannon realized she couldn't afford to stay in New York with no income. She decided to sell her beloved apartment in Tribeca, a beautiful place she had worked hard to afford and was proud to own. When her apartment sold, Shannon traveled to Europe for six weeks and then moved home to live near her parents in Chicago. This was October 2008, and as the Chicago winter closed in on her, Shannon holed up in her apartment, trying to regroup and figure out what she was going to do with the rest of her life.

"I did nothing for six months," she says. "Without a job and away from my friends and contacts in New York, I honestly had nothing to do. And I had no income. I would try to not go out of the house because I knew if I did I'd just spend money. It was a hard winter."

Looking for a way to pull herself out of the unemployment morass, Shannon decided to go back to school for a master's degree in real estate. She learned about a school in Chicago with a good program and won a scholarship. While going to school wasn't a paying job, Shannon told herself it was a reason to get up and get out of the house every morning, the kick in the pants that she needed to shake the doldrums.

"Going back to school gave me momentum," Shannon says. "I needed to get going with something again. I believe that once you get one good thing happening, other good things follow."

Around the same time that Shannon started her grad program, she also found part-time work at an auction house in Chicago. While the work wasn't related to any kind of work she'd ever done before, for the first time in months, Shannon felt satisfied, as if, in a few small ways, her life was regaining direction.

"The job was only two days a week," Shannon says, "but it was good for me. After being alone in my apartment for so many months, I was starved for a work environment." It was just an assistant's job, well below her qualifications, Shannon says. But it didn't matter. "I was doing completely menial tasks like moving things around and other kinds of labor. But I was interested in what I was doing and it was fun to be around people again. It wasn't about the money or the prestige. It was more about doing something I thought was interesting."

Lindgren often encourages her clients to take a part-time job while they are looking for a full-time position.

"I'm big on getting unemployed people into part-time jobs as quickly as possible, even if it isn't in their field," Lindgren says. "Even though you might feel like it is, doing something on the side is not a waste of your time. I don't think a person needs forty hours a week to do a job search, and I think part-time work helps open up the mind and lead to other opportunities."

Fueled by her positive momentum, Shannon completed her graduate degree. She decided she needed experience in international real estate, and so she applied for internships at brokerage firms in London. She landed two good spots and flew to England to complete the assignments back to back. The internships were great fun and good experience, but they didn't lead to a job. Reluctantly, Shannon packed up and headed back to the States.

"When I got back from London, I was really sad. I had nothing to do. I had no clue what to do. My twentieth high-school reunion was coming up. I had planned the event. During the reunion people would ask me, 'What are you doing these days?' I'd have to say, 'Well, nothing.' By then I was living with my parents in their guest room in Chicago. It was embarrassing for a person who'd always been so successful."

At this point, Shannon was closing in on her fourth year of unemployment. At one point, she thought she'd secured a job at a brokerage firm back in New York, but a younger associate somehow slipped in and managed to steal the job out from under her. Shannon was crushed.

"I was thrown under the bus," Shannon says. "It was heartbreaking because I'd mentored this guy and thought he was my friend."

Shannon began to focus her frustrated excess energy on exercise. "I had just started doing Bikram yoga," she tells me. "I got totally obsessed with it, in a good way. I ended up doing it all the time. I think it helped me because it was an hour and a half of focusing on what I was doing there and not thinking about anything that was going on outside. On the day I found out that I didn't get that job, I went to class. I felt horrible going in, but coming out I felt clearheaded. The distraction of yoga was good for me."

With clear breath filling her head and balancing in her mind, Shannon was overjoyed to get a call from a recruiter telling her that a Big Four advisory firm wanted to hire her as a manager. The job was in Washington, D.C., and when she was offered the position, Shannon was thrilled to make the move. She was more than ready to start the next chapter in her life, one that begins after she finished what she now likes to call her "four-year sabbatical."

"Surprisingly, I'm not jaded about what happened," she tells me. "I realize now that I'm a better person than I was before I lost my job. Before, I was working all the time. I was focused on my work at the expense of the rest of my life and my relationships. I was making good money back then, but I see now I wasn't all that interesting as a person. After spending all these years getting back on my feet, I have so much more perspective on life. I realize that I can always figure out ways to make money, but I may not always be able to figure out ways to be happy."

Survival tips for the unemployed:

✚ **Understand that being out of work happens to everyone, even career counselors.**

Lindgren is the rare breed of career counselor who will actually admit to having a less-than-spotless employment record. A gentle-voiced woman with a ready smile, she has held a variety of jobs and even been laid off—or fired—from a couple of them. Being approachable helps Lindgren's clients loosen up. "I know what it feels like to wake up unemployed," Lindgren laughs. "I'm not ashamed to admit it, and you shouldn't be either."

+ **Looking for work isn't a full-time job,** Karyn Frisch says. "I don't think a person needs forty hours a week to do a job search. It's not realistic."

Amy Lindgren agrees. "There are only so many hours you can spend calling and searching and writing résumés. If you devote all your waking hours to it, you won't find a job any sooner—and you will drive yourself crazy."

+ **Give yourself a break**. Take time off, visit museums, talk to friends and family, says Norm Elrod.

Elrod's wife has always encouraged him to make his life about more than looking for work. "When I didn't have a job, my wife would always tell me, 'Give yourself some time off,'" he says. "At first, I would spend all my time looking for jobs. I would put in long days. I was working hard. My wife said, 'Take some time off. Do something you want to do.' Some people might suggest going to the movies in the middle of the afternoon, but I found it depressing. Instead, I'd go to museums or even play some video games. That was my way of taking a little time for myself."

+ If you can afford it, **use your extra time for travel,** Shannon advises. Once you get another job, you will regret not taking this opportunity.

"If I knew someone who lost their job today," she says, "I'd tell them to make plans to travel and go see people who make them happy. If an opportunity came up for me to travel during my years of unemployment, I'd take it if I could afford it. And when people offered to put me up in their homes, I'd accept the offer. It helped me have something to look forward to, something that boosted my spirits."

+ Bob, Elrod and Shannon believe in the **power of exercise** as a tool for stress relief, improved self-confidence, and general health.

"For me, going to the gym was a great way to get some of that unemployment frustration out," Elrod laughs. "Let's just say I was in really good shape while I was unemployed. A great way to survive stress is to find your outlets and develop them. I think I found mine."

A longtime hockey player, Bob joined an adult league to burn energy while he was searching for a job. "Skating made me feel good, and the locker room camaraderie was good for my mental health. While I was looking for work, I'd play hockey two or three times a week. Now that I have a job, I still try to play at least once a week."

+ Expand a hobby or interest, Rusty advises.

"I've always been interested in car racing," he says. "When I had more time on my hands, I got out to the track and made myself available for pit crews. It was a great decision. I couldn't spend all my time mooning about not having a job. Working on the cars and making friends at the track helped me feel like I had a life of my own."

Bob joined his church's handbell choir while he was looking for work. He's still a member in good standing. "There are days I come home from work and I'm completely tense or pissed," he says. "Then I get into rehearsal and by the time I get to the second measure, something happens. The music turns off that pissed-off part of my brain. I get in a better place. Afterwards, I'll get in the car and I can't even remember the thing that was bothering me in the first place."

+ Develop a project that can lead to future employment, Norm urges.

Creating a website was a way for Elrod to build skills that made him more appealing to potential employers. And the extra time created by unemployment gave him time to teach himself the skills he needed to build a successful site. "It helped future employers look at me in a different light.

+ Be flexible and willing to move for work, says Taylor.

"Odds are, your dream job isn't sitting there in your back yard," she advises. "Keep your eyes open for opportunity. You may have to move to get the work you want. If you need work, you have to be willing to follow the jobs. Your dream job might not be where you are. Sometimes you just have to jump. You have to do what's needed to get the life you want."

✚ And, most important of all, Frisch and Lindgren insist that you **put job loss in perspective**.

"I always start my workshops by saying, 'Whatever reason you are out of work today doesn't matter anymore," Frisch says. "'You are now in a recovery phase, and it's my job to help you recover. Eventually, being out of a job will be just a memory.'"

Losing a job is a bummer, to be sure, but there are worse things that can happen, Lindgren believes. While she doesn't like to minimize her clients' trauma, she also likes to give them a baseline against which to measure the pain of job loss.

"When I first meet with people, I try to help put things in perspective," she smiles. "When they come in and they're really feeling traumatized about being out of work, I'll say, 'This seems to be taking a toll on you. On a scale of one to ten, does this seem to be the worst thing that has ever happened to you in your life?' Most people will say, 'God, no.' Then I'll ask, 'What was your hardest thing? How did you get through it?' People will tell me about their hardest life experience and how they made it through to the other side. Then I'll ask, gently, 'Have you thought how you might use some of those same coping skills to deal with unemployment?' It usually helps people realize that they have reserves of strength within themselves."

Chapter 6
How to Survive Debt, Bankruptcy, and Foreclosure

It was a house I'd passed by many times on my countless walks around the neighborhood. It looked sturdy, built around, say, 1915, and it had plenty of character—a tidy front porch, well-maintained wood siding, a cozy back yard—plus one attractive perk my own little house just two blocks away does not possess: a third floor.

One day a few years ago, a militia of bright-red *Open house! Bank-owned property!* signs went up. Coming home from an errand, I followed them. The open house turned out to be for *the* house, so I decided to take a look.

If my neighborhood walks have taught me anything, it's that in the last few years, many sturdy, charming houses just like this one have stayed on the market way too long, the "For Sale" signs in their front yards sprouting weeds. Eventually a jaunty little "Price Reduced" sign is added to the display; sometimes that's enough and the house is eventually sold for less than the seller hoped, but I've also watched as other homes sit unclaimed, like brave-faced girls standing at the edge of the dance floor, waiting for a partner. Nosy neighbor that I am, I decided to take a look around.

As I walked in the front door, I realized this was no ordinary open house. There was no polite "Please remove your shoes!" sign, no eager real estate agent standing by the dining room table, arranging a neat pile of brochures. Instead, there were two tough-looking guys with greasy ties. One had his foot propped on an upholstered dining room chair, elbow resting casually on his knee. It was a snowy day, and because visitors hadn't been asked to remove their boots, the floor was covered with muddy, gritty tracks.

The tracks led around the house, which, rather than being "staged" for a lucrative sale, looked more like the scene of a hasty getaway, or even an abduction. The family's food lined the shelves, piles of magazines and newspapers littered the floor, and upstairs the bedrooms seemed hastily abandoned, blankets askew. In one corner room, a feather pillow still held the telltale dent of its user's head. The third floor was unfinished and littered with half-opened boxes of belongings. A frightened cat hid in the corner. It felt like the home's occupants had been roused from their beds and told to clear out just minutes before the open-house signs went up. More likely, though, they just weren't all that keen about selling their home and had run out of options.

The best way to describe the scene is how my friend's real estate agent once summed up a cute (from the curb, at least) little bungalow with a destroyed interior. "Outside best side."

Whatever the story, even though it was obviously still home to someone's family, the house felt abandoned, weighed down by a heavy, gray cloud of sadness. It was impossible to imagine ever feeling happy there.

Back in the dining room, one of the guys was sweet-talking a young couple, saying, "You can probably get this place for at least $50,000 less than the asking price. The bank wants these people out." His buddy handed me a flier. "Here's a list of every bank-owned property located within a square mile of this place," he said. "There are a lot of foreclosures right now." He paused, and smiled, his eyes surveying the room. "This is a great opportunity. Prices haven't been this low in years."

Talk about making lemonade out of lemons. I cleared out of there as quickly as I could, but I couldn't shake the feeling of that abandoned-but-not-really-abandoned house, of the gritty footprints all over the floor, of the carelessly-pushed-aside possessions and the frightened cat, of capitalizing on another family's bad fortune.

These days, things are slowly starting to look up from when I first toured that house. And while US home foreclosure rates are slowly sliding down from the all-time high they hit this decade, you'd still have to be living in a cave not to realize that scenes like the one I witnessed are still happening in cities and towns everywhere: Since the onset of the housing crisis in September 2008, 4.2 million homes have been lost to foreclosure, estimates the financial data analysis firm CoreLogic. The crisis affects everyone. Lenders lose up to $50,000 on each foreclosure, and neighborhoods and city governments struggle to keep up revenues and pay for basic services when homes sit unoccupied for months on end. Crime rates rise and remaining homeowners lose value in their investments.

But the economic effects of foreclosure may be secondary to the emotional toll that accompanies the loss of a home. In a Harris Interactive poll of over 1,000 homeowners, 38 percent reported that the threat of foreclosure would make them feel scared, 35 percent said depressed, 9 percent said angry, and 8 percent said embarrassed.

"When people are facing foreclosure, that translates into facing the loss of their home," Darryl Dahlheimer, program director of Lutheran Social Service financial counseling in Minneapolis, says. He's sitting across from me in his tidy office, and as he talks, he leans forward in his chair, spreading his hands across his desktop. In these days of recovery from great economic upheaval, Dahlheimer says, a large percentage of clients in his nonprofit are still facing staggering credit card debt and home foreclosure. "The major emotions that go with that are fear and shame," he says. "The fear that comes from this experience is natural. It's the fear of being homeless. My clients are thinking, 'If the place where I sleep at night might go away, everything else could disappear.' It's a panicky sense of fear."

Call me oversensitive, but the foreclosed house I toured back then smelled like panic and fear. I've yet to be at risk of losing my house, but we all could be just a layoff or a serious illness away from desperate times.

How does a family end up under a cloud of bankruptcy and foreclosure, and how do they survive its aftermath? In this day and age, it's not hard to find people who are living through the experience, but what's harder to find are those who've made it through to the other side and emerged, stronger, wiser, and in control of their financial lives.

The leap: taken. The landing: hard.

Hindsight being 20/20, Craig and Sharon now believe that they never really felt *at home* in the house that they had to surrender to the bank back in 2007.

"Some houses you feel an emotional attachment to," says Sharon, a kind, mild-mannered freelance editor. "Some houses you don't. This house was one of those kinds of houses. We never felt an attachment to that neighborhood or to that house—not like we did to the house we owned before—so having to leave it behind wasn't the worst thing that ever happened to us."

But even if it wasn't the worst thing that ever happened to them, the process of going bankrupt and losing their home was traumatic for this long-married Minneapolis couple and their two then-teenage children. Through a risky combination of financing a lifelong dream and faith in the strength of the housing market, they managed to lose everything they'd worked for—from their savings to their credit rating, to their car, to the roof over their heads.

"I won't lie," says Craig, a magazine editor. "We all felt bruised by the experience. But we always knew we'd come out on the other side."

On the surface, Craig and Sharon don't fit the classic stereotype of failed American homeowners. They didn't buy themselves trouble in the form of an overpriced suburban mega-mansion, and they weren't first-time homebuyers wheedled into an unsafe transaction by shady lenders. What they were—and still are—is an idealistic couple who dare to dream big, who don't get too caught up in worries about financial "what ifs," who don't have a natural aptitude for business, and who don't spend a lot of time dwelling on the past.

Many foreclosure stories can be read as cautionary tales about acting on big dreams, though the kind of dreams that are acted upon vary widely. Self-described "old hippies" who struggle with a general ambivalence about affluence, Craig and Sharon found themselves in financial crisis after Craig launched what he felt was a carefully planned business venture.

For most of his adult life, Craig had dreamed of running his own newspaper. After college, he worked as an editor at a series of small newspapers and magazines, earning "semi-meager" wages, and laboring under high-maintenance bosses. Nearing fifty, he'd had his fill of working for others. He decided that the time was right to start his own publication, a weekly newspaper designed to rival his city's daily.

"I had big dreams then," Craig says. "I did a business plan. I talked to rich people, trying to get someone to invest. I thought I needed to raise $5 million." Craig met with potential investors. Many were frustrated with the city's news coverage and interested in seeing an alternative venue, but none—perhaps seeing print journalism's coming struggle—were interested in investing.

"What you said at the time was you were waiting for somebody to tell you that you *couldn't* do this," Sharon says to Craig.

"And nobody told me I *couldn't* do it," Craig says. "But nobody would give me the money, either."

Sharon reminds him, kindly. "Everybody was telling you it wasn't a viable idea, but you didn't want to hear that. Neither did I."

The lack of investor interest slowed progress on his newspaper to a crawl. Instead, Craig launched an e-mail newsletter based on his concept, and the print version was put on hold. But life goes on even when dreams are deferred, and in 1998, the family decided to sell their cramped two-bedroom home and move into a slightly more spacious four-bedroom. The price? A reasonable $130,000, but to a frugal couple used to surviving on a modest editor's salary, it felt like a small fortune.

"There was this sense of abundance and promise," Craig says. We're drinking tea in the family's back yard as the soft summer-evening light wanes. "I was making decent money at the time and we felt that we needed a bigger place to spread out in. The housing market was strong. We thought we should try."

"At that point in time was the beginning stages of the real estate boom," Sharon adds. "There was this sense that you should buy the most house you can qualify for because it could only go up in value, so it's a good investment."

Everybody was doing it

As they saw housing values rise, Craig and Sharon watched as their friends began refinancing their homes, squeezing value out of what felt like a solid investment. Craig began to wonder if maybe he didn't need an investor for his newspaper after all. Maybe the equity in his family's home could provide the seed money to get his dream off the ground.

"Remember when we had the big house and we had one mortgage?" Craig says. Sharon nods and smiles. "Everybody was refinancing and we'd never done that. We felt like we were behind, like we were missing out, like we were schlumps. Everybody was doing it. I'd talk to someone on the phone and they'd be like, 'Whoa. We just refinanced at 5 percent. It was so awesome. You really need to do this.'"

So they did it, first refinancing the house to pay for their daughter's braces. Then, a little over a year later, they returned to the bank and negotiated a home-equity loan to start the newspaper. Screwing up his courage to take the leap, Craig quit his day job.

"They say successful entrepreneurs are good at hedging their bets," Sharon says. "You could argue we were not successful entrepreneurs, but we were very optimistic. We really believed there was a need for this newspaper and we really believed there was a market niche, that people were going to want to reach our hip, urban readers." But ad sales were distressingly slow and the weekly format quickly became too costly to maintain, Sharon tells me. Within three weeks, the free weekly morphed into a monthly.

The harsh reality is that even from its earliest days, Craig and Sharon's paper was doomed. It's expensive to produce a publication, and when revenues don't support costs, something has to give. Though they lost money on every single issue, Craig and Sharon produced their paper for almost two years. They never drew salaries for themselves, instead paying writers, printers, and others directly out of their home-equity line, and later, after that money ran out, from advances on their personal credit cards. The hole they were digging got deeper and deeper. Then the walls started caving in.

"We talked about 'Should we shut it down?' and we'd say, 'No, no, no. We can't,' until there was just no way to keep it going," Sharon recalls. "And by that time I, too, could see that we needed to do this. And so we stopped. The last issue was December 2005. Craig took a realistic look at our finances at that point and said, 'We need to meet with a bankruptcy attorney.'"

At this point, the couple was more than $100,000 in debt. Because she wanted to pay back everything they owed, Sharon resisted bankruptcy for more than six months. They took odd jobs, scrambling to keep up with their payments. The interest on their credit cards kept compounding, and the pressure was too much. When a credit card company that promised to consolidate their debt instead added another high-interest credit card to their account, Sharon was ready to give up—even if "giving up" meant giving up their house.

"I was pissed, basically," she recalls, shaking her head grimly. "I was mad and I said, 'Fine. Screw 'em all. Let's meet with the bankruptcy attorney.'"

It's everybody's problem

Bankruptcy and foreclosure don't happen in isolation. Because— and this is the very reality that kept Sharon fighting to keep up with payments for all those months—when an individual steps away from his or her financial responsibilities, all those to whom he or she owes money are stuck with the bill. Because the cycle is self-perpetuating (creditor becomes debtor and on and on), the impact of a personal financial implosion is felt in the community at large.

Some of those unpaid bills are actual—Sharon was never able to completely pay the printer all the money they owed, for instance. Other unpaid bills are more metaphorical—bankruptcy and foreclosure inflict psychological damage on homeowners, leaving many in a nearly frozen state of anger, hopelessness, and self-pity.

When he sees one of his clients moving in this direction, Dahlheimer tries to step in and redirect.

"People often feel they were misled by mortgage brokers who put them in a home they couldn't afford," he says. "We also hear lots of anger directed at lenders and at the sheriffs who are putting people out of their homes. They feel like someone ought to help them."

People have a right to their emotions, Dalheimer believes, but in many cases their anger is misplaced. When a stressed homeowner portrays himself or herself as a helpless "victim" of the real estate Ponzi scheme, Dalheimer reminds them that they were willing players in the transaction. Sure, during the worst of the crisis, irresponsible lenders preyed on uninformed homebuyers, but putting all the blame on others and casting oneself as a faultless victim gets a person nowhere.

The first step toward financial (and by limited extension, emotional) healing is accepting responsibility for a share of your troubles, Dalheimer says, learning how to make some changes, and then hopping into the driver's seat and charting your own course for financial independence.

"For the last 20 years, Americans have been fed the line that everybody deserves to own a home," Dalheimer tells me. Sounds good, but the truth is that "homeownership is not the right financial decision for everyone. Not everyone can afford it. I coach people to look at all their options and make realistic housing choices. Sometimes that means letting the house go. Usually it means cutting up the credit cards. Sometimes we have to start over."

Starting over doesn't have to be the worst thing that ever happened. Financial advisor Ruth Hayden, author of *For Richer, Not Poorer: The Money Book for Couples,* says that she advises her clients to put money—and the possessions it can buy—in perspective. Financial hardship can be devastating, but it's not the end of your life.

"The important thing to remember with foreclosure is this: It's just money," Hayden says. "You can even say 'It's just a house.' It's not the end of the world. You will recover. In this capitalistic system, losing money is portrayed as the same as losing a loved one, but it's not. Money is just money. Other things are more important." For many Americans, accepting—and embracing—that reality can be extremely difficult.

Gambling on happiness

Several years ago, Julia, her husband, Todd, and their two young daughters lived in the countryside outside of Austin, Texas, in a three-room cabin that once belonged to her grandfather.

Julia describes the place for me like this: "It's small, and pretty basic with drop-panel ceilings and pre-fab kitchen cabinets. But it was much, much better than nothing."

And nothing had actually been an option for this family, when the ocean of debt they were swimming in threatened to pull them under and forced them to flee their 3,500-square-foot home in the Austin suburbs, situated, according to Julia, "On a big corner lot in a golf course community." When Julia talks about her former house, her deep feelings of pride seep through. "It had four bedrooms, three living rooms, a separate office, and a separate formal dining room with a huge kitchen," she says. "It had a ton of perks. In many ways, it really is my dream house."

The family's financial troubles all seemed to start simply enough. Julia owned a modest home when she and Todd married and began trying to start a family. But having children proved more difficult than the couple imagined. They decided to terminate their first pregnancy at twenty-two weeks, after learning during a routine ultrasound that the fetus suffered from a rare congenital disorder. Then they subsequently lost two more children to miscarriage.

"We so wanted to have a child," Julia tells me. "When it looked like we couldn't, we started spending."

Their first—and biggest—purchase was the "dream house." Then, because the house was so big, Julia, a freelance marketing writer, and Todd, a real estate agent, felt they had to buy furniture to fill every room. And they decided that their big yard needed professional landscaping—and a new limestone patio to go with it. They charged most of these purchases on credit cards.

"A lot of the debt we got ourselves into came as a result of grief spending," Julia says. "After our first loss, I quit my job, and we were living on Todd's income. But we kept spending—and building up debt. It was the direct consequence of trying to cheer ourselves up, to medicate ourselves with material belongings." And in Julia and Todd's circle of friends, rewarding and comforting oneself with material goods was the norm. Their friends all lived in impeccably furnished new homes that were just as large as or larger than theirs. Their children had big, fancy birthday parties and wore brand-new clothes. Julia and Todd felt pressure to keep up.

When the couple finally managed to conceive and give birth to a child, their first daughter arrived mostly healthy but a bit early, and required a one-week stay in the NICU. Insurance covered much of the bill, but the couple was still left owing the hospital thousands of dollars. In the meantime, they took in Todd's ill mother and took out a home-equity loan to finance her care. Then, three years later, they had a second daughter.

It was a bad time to be a young, growing family. The housing market in Austin seized up and Todd told his wife that his real estate business was drying up to nearly nothing. For six months after their second daughter was born, he didn't sell a single house, and the couple again pulled out their credit cards. The family's debt began to pile up and up, eventually leaving them at a point where they were spending two-thirds of their income on credit card payments.

It was a horrible, stressful period. Keeping up with their debt load made paying the mortgage impossible. Realizing that they were in eminent danger of losing their house, Julia and Todd decided to find a renter for their home, sell everything that wouldn't fit in the cabin ("That was most of everything," Julia laughs), pack up their daughters, and move out to the country. Julia's grandfather had offered to let the family stay in the cabin rent-free for three years— while they promised to work to right their financial ship.

For months—years, even—Todd told everyone, including his wife, that the family's financial problems were solely the fault of the economy. Once the real estate market started building steam again, things would look up, he promised: They just needed to tighten their belts for now. Julia trusted her husband, and drastically altered her spending habits. She cut up her credit cards, stopped buying new clothes for herself and her daughters, signed up with a counselor at the local branch of Consumer Credit Counseling Service, and even approached their church for help paying the grocery bills.

For Julia, these felt like huge steps. "It took a lot of courage for me to step forward and ask for help," she tells me. "I'd been living in some sort of fantasy for too long, and I thought we were finally being honest, finally setting things right."

The truth will set you free

Renting out the house and living payment-free was a wise financial step for Todd and Julia, says Dalheimer. Too often, he sees clients whose fight to continue living in a house they can't afford leaves them worse off than ever. Sometimes it's better to move out and move on.

"We coach people to look at all their options to make realistic housing choices now that they are behind," he says. "Sometimes that means letting the house go. I help my clients prepare for whatever transition there is by having realistic conversations about what options are feasible." If a rent-free housing option exists, Dalheimer would surely advise his clients to make the step—but once the move is made, there are other things that need to be done. "If someone is going to lose their home, it's always a good idea to prepare for a Plan B. If they move out of their home, we need to figure out what they will do as a renter to get the rest of their finances in order—to focus on how to not get out of the frying pan and back into the fire."

But the sorry truth was that during the family's tough period of so-called belt-tightening, Todd was actually spending more than ever. After a little snooping, Julia—who'd left financial concerns up to her husband—discovered that Todd's real estate career had been mostly a sham: A gambling addict, he'd been siphoning money out of the family's savings to fuel his poker addiction, maxing out credit cards, drawing down his daughters' college savings plans, and even taking out loans.

"He was taking anywhere from $2,000 up to $7,000 a month in cash out of our accounts," Julia says to me. "All that time, I was working nonstop to try to keep us afloat. He was supposedly a real estate agent, but he was only doing that as a front to gamble."

After Julia discovered what had been going on, her marriage fell apart. And when Todd finally moved out, Julia was left to patch up the family's troubled finances alone. Her relationship with her Consumer Credit Counseling advisor became even more important. After a long meeting where Julia outlined her new stack of financial problems, the counselor stepped in with assistance and advice. The first step was to help Julia take charge of her skyrocketing credit card debt, working with the credit card companies to negotiate a managed payment plan. Determined to clean up her credit history so she could start her new life on a more financially stable note, Julia, a hardworking, committed achiever, stuck religiously to her counselor's recommendations.

"I buckled down and made a very large monthly payment," Julia says. It wasn't easy, and it took her more than two years to meet her goal, continuing with the "super-thrifty" financial behavior she'd learned to develop at the beginning of her family's economic downturn. "I didn't own credit cards," she says. "If I didn't have cash to pay for something, I didn't buy it." During that period, Julia and her daughters didn't go out to eat, didn't take vacations, and they only bought secondhand.

Today, Julia's life is completely different from where it was before her family's financial meltdown. "I've paid off every last bit of debt associated with my ex," she says. "Being a single mom was horrible. But thanks to my consumer credit counselor, I was able to split the debt out according to whose name was on which credit card. In the end, I paid off $22,000 in credit card debt and about $18,000 in income taxes. The rest is my ex-husband's responsibility. I'm really, really proud that I was able to accomplish that."

Julia's remarried now, with a stepdaughter and a new baby boy. She views her past life as just that. In the past. She and her new husband focus on living within their means. They also maintain a transparent approach to managing family finances; they promised each other that they'd work together to keep the books balanced and never make a major financial decision without talking it through.

With her debt cleared up and her relationship finally on honest, firm footings, Julia feels like she's in a better place than ever. But she still keeps a memory of her past financial stumblings.

"You do have a choice to make after something traumatic happens," Julia says. "You have a choice of where you go from there." One choice, she says, is to burrow down into the trauma and never get out, wasting time and energy blaming others for your situation. Or, Julia tells me, resolutely, you can take responsibility for your life and dig yourself out. "That's the approach I've chosen to take in my life."

And now that she's ensconced in her new, financially responsible life, Julia makes a point to provide support for others who are in the same situation she found herself in. She reaches out to folks experiencing financial meltdown, telling them about her own experiences and suggesting they seek credit counseling to turn their financial lives around. "I want to let people know that even though it may feel like you are drowning in debt, you can pull yourself out of it and make things right again," she says. "I am an example of that."

It's essential that we see people like Julia, people whose lives have been turned upside down by the financial crisis and are facing their problems with courage.

"In the media there is a tremendous push for stories that pull at heartstrings, that describe people as 'victims of this,' or 'victims of that.' It's all about hand-wringing and very little about taking charge, taking full responsibility, and solving the problem yourself. What needs to be highlighted is that managing to solve these problems are stories of true *survival*—not just heartwarming stories we can all learn from, but true-life tales of real, ordinary people who deserve our respect for doing the hard work of facing up to their responsibilities."

Broke—but not broken

Craig and Sharon went bankrupt and lost their house not because they were busy buying *things* or keeping up with the Joneses, but because they were single-mindedly focused on fulfilling a dream. When they finally realized that they'd bitten off much more than they could chew, they adjusted their dream. Instead of continuing to publish a monthly paper, they switched gears and created a quarterly literary journal. These days, they've whittled that dream down even further, publishing and distributing a small annual calendar to a select audience of diehard fans. This product bears only a passing resemblance to the project that turned out to be their financial downfall, but in a world of real-life grown-up responsibilities, it still provides a small outlet for their creative spirits.

Going bankrupt was less traumatic for Craig and Sharon and their children than the experience is for many Americans. Sharon theorizes that her family's fall from economic grace maybe hurt less than others' because they didn't actually have all that far to fall.

"When we were first married we were so broke we didn't buy a marriage license," she tells me. "We couldn't afford rings back then and we still don't have them because we've never gotten around to it. Stuff like that just doesn't matter to us. In fact, we've nearly been in foreclosure before but somehow we got out of it. Once we almost had to borrow money from Craig's dad to pay the heating bill." At this memory, Sharon smiles almost wistfully. "At the end of all this mess, my feeling was 'We've been there, done that. No big deal if we go broke.' We've been broke. We know what that's like. We have a lot of experience at being broke."

But for all of their cavalier talk about the disintegration of their finances, the idea of losing their home was a source of stress for the couple and their children. For a long time after they went bankrupt, they fought to keep their house, but when it was clear that their debts were too much, that they'd never be able to make another mortgage payment, Craig and Sharon despaired—briefly. Then a friend of their daughter's who had fixed up a small home for quick resale offered to rent the place to their family with no credit checks.

The couple—who tend to believe in omens both good and bad— jumped at what looked like a temporary safe harbor. They packed up their possessions and moved into the rental. Suddenly getting out before the bank kicked them out seemed mighty appealing.

"I wouldn't have gone back to the house," says Sharon. "It would have been too weird. I wouldn't have wanted to see the neighbors. It would've been uncomfortable."

While their former home sat abandoned, Sharon tells me that she and Craig would "drive by it every once in a while." She adds, "It was more a matter of curiosity. I wanted to see if anyone was living in it yet. I felt bad for my neighbors. I felt guilty that we had left an empty house on the street for such a long time. Other people in our situation probably wouldn't have moved out as quickly as we did, but part of our anxiety was that we had a dog and three cats and when we had the opportunity to rent a house, we jumped at it. We also fully expected that by the end of that year it would be all done."

A year after his financial meltdown, Craig snapped up a good-paying job as managing editor of a national magazine. "To be fair, as much as we enjoy our current affluence," says Sharon, "we're still a tiny bit ambivalent about affluence in general." But it didn't take long for them to adjust to this change in financial standing. With a steady paycheck coming in the door, they were able to get a head start on putting their financial house in order. And a few years later, they bought a neat, cozy house not far from their rental.

In the end, things didn't really change much for Craig and Sharon. They lost the bigger house—but that was OK. Sharon believes that their family ties were strengthened by the upheaval, that they were able to strip away all the excess (not that there was all that much excess to begin with) and focus on each other, and creating a happy, peaceful life. They have no regrets about what happened. In fact, they believe it was meant to be.

Survival tips for the bankrupt from people who've been there:

+ **Keep credit spending to a minimum,** Julia says. "When our financial problems started to get bad, my first husband and I pulled out the credit cards," she says. In the end, compounding debt from those over-extended cards was what put the couple over the financial edge.

"Take a deep breath and cut up those cards," she says. "And live on cash only. It's the fastest, safest way to keep yourself out of debt."

+ Julia learned this the hard way, but she now stresses the **importance of open, honest financial communication between couples**. "All married women need to understand their financial situation," she says now. "Since it happened to me, I've heard from a lot of powerful women who hand off all of their family's financial dealings to their husbands." It can sound appealing to have someone else take care of your finances, Julia says, but putting your head in the sand is a risky idea. "Both members should know what's in the bank. Then, if things start getting tricky, both of you can work together to straighten things out." Financial advisor and author Ruth Hayden couldn't agree more.

+ Craig and Sharon still believe in the importance of daring to live your dreams but **advise dreamers to start small**. It turned out that mortgaging their house to finance a weekly newspaper was far too risky an approach that put their personal finances in jeopardy. "We should have tried out starting smaller with fewer issues and then built the paper from there," Craig says. "A more conservative approach might have been wiser."

+ **Before financial problems hit a breaking point, seek advice from a certified credit counselor**, Dahlheimer suggests. Julia agrees. "Working with a credit counselor was the best thing I ever did. He helped me feel like I was finally in control of my financial life when my mounting debt had made me feel like I was totally out of control."

+ **Craig and Sharon remind others to put priorities in order:** Family, friends, and experiences first, possessions a distant second. "We've always thought that things aren't important at all," Sharon says. "Owning lots of stuff has always been a low priority. And that's a good thing, because when we lost the stuff we had, it didn't hurt us so much. We were OK. Our kids were OK. Losing our house didn't really hurt all that much."

Chapter 7

How to Survive the Death of a Child

When she was thirty-one, Ann, one of my closest childhood friends, died of bone cancer. She was buried in a quiet cemetery on a lake just outside the small town where she grew up, married, and raised her daughter.

A few years ago, my elderly uncle died, and I was back at that same cemetery for his memorial service. Later, after the mourners had drifted away, I went off to look for Ann's grave. It was right where I'd remembered it, a thick granite stone inscribed with Ann's name and the years she was born and died. As I reached over to place my hand on the sun-warmed stone, I saw another, newer marker. The gravestone bore Ann's mother's name. She'd died eight years after her daughter.

Those side-by-side gravestones, daughter and then mother, troubled me. I remember Ann's mom, Joanne, as a hardworking, sassy wisecracker, a parent who'd decorated their small house for every holiday, who'd had a laugh like a barking seal, who'd doted on her only daughter.

On birthdays and Christmas, Ann's mom bought her what looked to my young eyes like mountains of presents. While my busy mother thought one sweater was sufficient, Ann's mom bought her three—in different colors, plus matching socks. Their modest house had two bedrooms and a partially finished attic. Ann and her parents occupied the bedrooms; her two brothers' room was in the attic.

I still remember when Ann's parents bought her a canopy bed. A grade-school girl's dream, the white-and-blue beauty was purchased on something exciting called *layaway*; when the bed was finally delivered, Ann's dad set it up in her room. It looked like a princess's chamber.

Decades later, Ann died in that very same room. I visited her house on the day she passed; I can't remember if Ann lay dying in her canopy bed or in a rented hospital one, but I do remember Joanne, her eyes red and tired. She was standing in the kitchen, by the sink, taking a break or getting a glass of water, when I came in the back door. As Ann grew sicker and weaker, visitors had been coming and going for days. I hadn't seen Joanne since I'd graduated from high school and left for college, so I wasn't sure if she remembered me, but I handed her two old photos of Ann I'd taken back in high school. In both, Ann was smiling her wide, goofy grin. She looked young, healthy, and vigorous.

In the other room, my old friend was in bed, her breathing slow and shallow. I sat next to her for fifteen or twenty minutes and thanked her for being my friend. I put my hand on hers, told her I'd miss her, that the world would be a sadder place without her.

Later, as I was leaving, Joanne looked at my pictures and sighed. "It's so hard," she said, gruffly, rubbing her eyes with the back of her hand. And that was all. I never talked to her again.

What happened? Ann's dad, Don, is a quiet, soft-spoken man who still lives in the same house where his daughter died. He retired from his factory job years ago, and since his wife passed away, his life has been quiet. When I ask him about what happened to Joanne, Don's answer is simple.

"She was never the same after Ann died," he tells me. Joanne lived eight years longer than her daughter, but, Don adds, "after Ann, it was like she just kinda gave up."

Ann's cancer was cruel and painful, with chemotherapy, radiation, and, ultimately, major amputations. Joanne was there for her every moment of the ordeal. Because Ann could no longer climb the stairs to her bedroom in the home she shared with her husband and daughter, she moved the few blocks back to her childhood home when she entered hospice, taking up residence in her old room on the first floor.

On the day of my visit, Ann died several hours after I left. Her family was by her side. Joanne, who brought Ann into the world, was also there to help her leave it.

"That was a tough one to bear," Don says, his voice faltering. "It's heck watching a child die."

Out of order

Pat Loder understands more than anyone that the death of a child feels terribly, painfully wrong. In 1991, when her children were five and eight, they were killed in a car accident. Loder, who was driving the car, survived.

For months and years after the accident, Loder and her husband struggled to right their worlds. Nothing felt normal and it felt like it never would again.

"For a parent, having a child die is out of the natural order of things," Loder tells me one quiet morning. "We expect that we are going to bury our grandparents or our parents. We even make plans for those events. We make a will and buy life insurance in case our spouse dies before us. But losing a child is such an unthinkable that your mind never goes there."

Even after the accident, Loder continued to avoid such thoughts. The car was struck by a speeding motorcycle, and while she suffered only minor injuries, both of her children were trapped in the car. As she waited for the ambulance, Loder says, she never even thought that her children's injuries could be fatal.

"Here I am bleeding and sitting on the side of the road," she tells me. "I knew my children were unconscious in that car. I never, never thought they were going to die. My mind did just not go there. As a mother you just don't think, 'My child might die.' You are the one that sits there and holds them during the night when they are sick. You don't think, 'My child could die.' This was the unnatural order of things."

But both of Loder's children did die, her son at the scene, and her daughter in a hospital hours later. The experience was utterly devastating, and for weeks Loder and her husband, Wayne, could barely function.

"After the children died, my day was spent rolled up in a ball on my bed or on the floor in the living room," Loder recalls. "I would just cry and cry."

It was during this time that someone told Loder's husband about Compassionate Friends, an international organization for bereaved parents. The couple owned a hardware store, and a customer dropped off a "Dear Abby" clipping about the group. There was a chapter in a nearby town that met monthly.

Loder wasn't interested. "My feeling at the time was 'Take me anyplace but don't take me there,'" she tells me, "because I felt that if I went to a meeting like that I was going to be asked to relive the worst day of my life. That was not a day that I wanted to share with anyone. I was a very private person and sharing the details of the worst day of my life, all of the thoughts, feelings, flashbacks I was having felt intimate and scary. I didn't think there was anything that was ever going to help me get better."

But eventually, after much discussion, the Loders decided to go to a Compassionate Friends meeting. At first, they weren't sure they found any benefit.

"I had built a high wall around myself," Loder says. She built the wall partly because she felt like the help that others were offering did nothing but hurt. Nobody understood what she was going through.

"After the death of a child, friends and family want to help you," Loder tells me. "They want you to be the old you again. But you can't be the old you anymore."

Her life would never be the same, and other people didn't want to accept that.

"The old me was the mom who built her life around her two children. When you are at work, you plan for when your children come home from school and day care, and all of a sudden a trip to the grocery store became a horrendous thing. You have to cook for two, no longer four. They are no longer there. You become this jumble of trying to find out who the new you is. At the same time, you are also trying to desperately hold on to the old you. When your children die, you think maybe you can get back the old you, but you can't because your life is so different. And nobody understands."

After attending several Compassionate Friends meetings, however, Loder began to meet people who understood. "I remember sitting in a meeting. This lady starting talking about the videotape that kept playing in her head, the one that shows her child's death. I thought, 'Oh, my gosh. Somebody else has that videotape going on in her head!' That's how it was for me. I'd feel the crash. I'd hear the metal against metal. I'd feel that slow-motion feeling when the car moved. I would wake up screaming at night. This videotape just wouldn't shut off in my head."

To know that there was somebody else out there who had the same experience was a revelation, Loder continues. "After that, I started to listen at meetings and I started to see that I wasn't alone in this journey, that other people had survived and I could survive, too. The fact that we could share how we felt and where we were on our journey at a Compassionate Friends meeting was very helpful."

Thirteen years ago, Jeremy Shatan, executive director of the New York–based Hope and Heroes Children Cancer Fund, lost his two-year-old son Jacob to brain cancer. Jacob's death shook Shatan and his wife to the core. He wrote about the experience in an essay that was published in the *New York Times* blog *Motherlode*. Even though time has helped him put Jacob's loss into perspective, Shatan wrote, he will never fully recover from the pain.

"I knew from the moment Jacob died that we would never get over his loss; we would only learn to live with it," Shatan's essay continues. "At the risk of torturing grammar, perhaps I should revise that mantra to be 'we would only be learning to live with it,' because it's a process that never stops."

That reality doesn't mean that Shatan and his wife haven't survived their loss. Since their oldest child died, they have gone on raising their two surviving children, living normal lives. But the memory of their specific loss lingers. To describe their state of being, Shatan and his wife have come up with a new term: High-Functioning Bereaved Parents.

Shatan says it to me this way: To be a high-functioning bereaved parent means that even though his son is dead, Shatan continues to live his life, working around and through the pain. While he and his wife have never forgotten their son or let go of him, they have also focused on moving on and living life as normally as possible. This included deciding to go ahead with building their family—even while Jacob was undergoing punishing treatments for his brain tumor.

"Some people thought we were crazy," Shatan tells me from his home in Manhattan. "My wife got pregnant when Jacob was still in treatment." In the face of death, for Shatan and his family, life went on. "Just the same way we'd put Jacob down for a nap when he was in the hospital, just as we disciplined and raised him like we would at any time, we also continued with our lives. We had a plan for our family that included more than one child. We stuck to our plans."

Their daughter, Hannah, was born six months before Jacob died. Their youngest son, Noah, never knew his brother.

"We are not hiding anything, but we are moving through the world in a way that people wouldn't necessarily know that you'd had a tragedy," Shatan says. "This identity has been something to hang on to, even when we feel we aren't functioning as well as we could."

Not long after Jacob died, Shatan and his wife tried bringing their then-infant daughter to a retreat for bereaved parents. The experience was intense, Shatan says. "We went to the retreat in August," Shatan tells me. "Jacob had died in June, and so we were really raw." At the retreat, Shatan's wife experienced a crippling migraine, and the couple thought about packing up and leaving. But they stuck it out and in the retreat discovered the strength that can be achieved by listening to others who have suffered a similar fate. After that weekend, they realized that they weren't alone in their loss.

"Anybody who's gone through that feels so different than their peers," Shatan says. "Suddenly you've seen too much. You've been through too much. It ages you. Your friends with healthy, live children, they don't understand what you are going through. To be with a group of people who really get it, who have similar stories, is very powerful."

For years after that first retreat, a friend suggested that Shatan and his wife and children consider attending Camp Sunshine, a free retreat in Maine designed for children and their families dealing with life-threatening illnesses and their impact. Camp Sunshine holds several different sessions year-round, with some weeks dedicated to families facing different types of cancer, transplants, lupus, sickle cell anemia, and other illnesses. Some sessions are focused specifically on bereavement.

"Our friend would keep saying, 'You guys gotta come. You guys gotta come,'" Shatan says. "We eventually decided to give it a try and it turned out to be amazing." Today, Shatan and his family spend time at Camp Sunshine twice a year.

The experience has made a tremendous impact on the family's life. At camp, Shatan's younger children get to spend time enjoying special children's programming; Shatan and his wife can attend parents' support sessions—or just relax and spend time alone with each other.

"Since Jacob's death, we have been careful not to make our younger kids' lives all about their dead brother," Shatan tells me. "But we also want to keep him as an important part of our family. We talk about him. We have pictures of him. He is still very much part of the family." At Camp Sunshine, this honest approach feels normal and healthy. "The idea that we can all go to a place where everybody else in the room has had a similar experience is really huge."

Even so many years later, meeting people at different stages of the grief process has also been helpful. "It's good to see people who are further along than you are. It also helps to help people who are newly bereaved. Often, when we come to camp, they will introduce us to a family who is there for the first time. They'll say, 'Sit with them at the dinner table. You can be a support for them, and offer a helping hand.' To be able to offer a helping hand and show somebody an example of survival has been healing for us."

Loder and her husband had a similar experience with Compassionate Friends. Hearing the stories of other bereaved parents helped put their own unique loss into perspective. And witnessing the healing of others also helped in their own healing.

"Often you will hear from a newly bereaved parent that their child who died is the first thing they think about in the morning and the last thing they think about at night," Loder tells me. For years, it was that way for Loder, and then, she says, her thinking changed, subtly.

"I remember where I was standing at this point in my life when I made the shift," she says. "I was standing in my bedroom and I thought, 'I feel different today.' This was three years down the road. I remember thinking that I felt different and then I realized that I hadn't thought about my children yet that morning. It almost felt like a weight had been lifted off my shoulders. It must've been a turning point, a healing point for me. I was still thinking about them all the time. But suddenly I realized a few hours had gone by and I hadn't thought about them yet." Loder had become a High-Functioning Bereaved Parent.

Though the burden of losing a child shifts and lightens over the years, the pain never completely goes away, Loder says. While other people may expect you to "get better" or "get over" the loss of your child, people who've lived through the experience understand. Even after all these years, that's one of the things she most appreciates about Compassionate Friends.

"I think the fact that when you are with other members—we don't want anybody else to join our club—they understand the fact that it would be my daughter's thirtieth birthday this year. After all this time, that was still a very melancholy time for me. To share that with somebody outside the group, they look at you like 'You are still talking about your dead child? Really?' After some time, people don't want you to talk about this. We are a death-denying society. To talk about a child that has died is really uncomfortable for people. So when you are around other Compassionate Friends, they understand and they will listen to how you feel about that day, that year, whatever."

On a mission

Before Jacob's death, Shatan and his wife worked as freelance photographers. They'd built a successful business, with a full client list and significant professional recognition. But after Jacob died, Shatan lost interest in his career.

Taking pictures didn't feel appealing anymore. His clients, focused on deadlines and assignments, didn't understand the depth of his grief. In the shadow of his loss, his work—maybe even his whole world—felt unimportant, superficial. Shatan realized he wanted a career where he could make a difference in the lives of others.

During Jacob's treatment, Shatan and his wife had become involved with the Children's Brain Tumor Foundation. The organization helped the family, and when Shatan found out that they wanted to hire a fundraiser, he applied for the job. The organization hired him, even though he had no prior experience.

"They took a chance on me," he laughs. "They hired me in May 2001. The dinner dance—their biggest fundraiser—was in June. It was a bit of a trial by fire, the school of fundraising hard knocks."

From that experience, Shatan's interest in cancer philanthropy grew. When he became executive director of the Hope & Heroes Cancer Fund, the fundraising arm of the Herbert Irving Child & Adolescent Oncology Center at Columbia University Medical Center, his work morphed into a true vocation.

"The necessity to make some kind of meaning out of Jacob's life and what happened to us was very strong," he says. "If I had been wealthy, maybe I would've become a big donor, but we weren't, so I did the next best thing. I donated myself."

The job felt right, Shatan says. "I wanted to be helping other people and I wanted to do something concrete that would help other families of children with cancer or brain tumors. For me, this is far more than a career."

At Hope & Heroes, Shatan's office is in the hospital's outpatient clinic. He tells me he's never found it hard to spend his days surrounded by children with cancer and their families. Maybe it was his experience caring for his son, but he feels comfortable there.

"For me it works," Shatan says. "I feel comfortable there. It is a hopeful place. It is a positive place, not a depressing place."

As the years have passed since their children's deaths, Loder and her husband became deeply involved in Compassionate Friends, eventually starting a chapter in their hometown. Then the pair became involved at the international level. They volunteered to edit the organization's twin newsletters, turning them into one magazine, *We Need Not Walk Alone*. In 2000, Loder became the executive director of the Illinois-based Compassionate Friends USA.

For Loder, involvement in Compassionate Friends has been more than a career—it is a sure source of healing. She mostly credits the opportunity to help others. "During chapter training sessions, we always try to tell people that helping is healing," Loder says. "When you see someone come into a chapter meeting and they are so raw and their grief is so fresh, then you'll see them turn a small corner and they'll reach out to someone else, you can actually see a transformation when they are helping someone along with their grief process."

Living life without her children is not always easy. But Loder believes that building on her experiences of grief has made her a stronger person.

"I've taken the worst thing that's ever happened to me and built it into my life," Loder says. "Instead of reliving it every day of my life, every second of my life, I don't think anymore so much about how my children died but rather how they lived and what great joy they continue to bring me in my life. Sometimes people will say, 'The grief is so tremendous I wish I never had my child.' I could never feel that way. My children taught me so much in life and in death. That is why I have reached out to other people who have experienced a similar situation."

Loder knows she is a different person today than she would have been had her children lived to adulthood. Some days she is even willing to say that living through her own personal trauma made her a better person. It hurts to say it, but she believes it to be true.

"I think that a lot of times we do not come out shiny from trauma," Loder tells me, "but we do come out new. In that newness, we become a better person."

Kind of like a moth coming out of a cocoon, Loder adds, pausing. Then she continues, slowly. "When my children died, I changed in a heartbeat, but I believe I am a more compassionate, more understanding person today because my children lived—*and* because they died. As you go through the process of mourning a child and begin to heal and mend, your grief is an open wound. You can pick the scab off and it starts to bleed. But when it scabs over again you are stronger. Stronger than ever before."

After her six-year-old daughter Abbey's death in a freak swimming-pool accident, Katey Taylor struggled to make sense of her life. Her active, sassy little girl had been playing in a country-club kiddy pool one summer evening when she was disemboweled by an uncovered pool drain. Remarkably, Abbey survived her injuries and even lived through a small-bowel, liver, and pancreas transplant. She died less than a year later from a rare transplant-related cancer.

Taylor changed after Abbey died. "I think I'm a very different person today than I was in June 2007," she tells me now. "I don't want to say I'm a harder person, but maybe I'm more calloused, guarded, cautious. I certainly am a very different person, but I also am trying my best to use what has happened to me and the skills that God gave me through this."

For Taylor, getting through the aftermath of her daughter's death involved trying to make something good out of tragedy. In 2012, she and her husband created Abbey's Hope, a nonprofit organization dedicated to pool safety and education.

"It didn't happen right away," Taylor says, "but eventually, after I'd gotten past the most painful part of the grief, I had this strong desire to help other children, to do everything I could to make sure something like this didn't happen to another child."

Taylor has three surviving daughters. "Pre-2007, I think I was a pretty good mom," she says to me, "but post-Abbey, there were some gray years." Taylor believes her youngest children missed out on her full attention during that gray time. Now she's working to make up lost time. "I'd say I'm doing my best now for my younger two. I'm working to be present in their lives and to show them the joy of life instead of living in a dark place. But it can be hard sometimes."

Taylor says her turning point came when her then-three-year-old daughter discovered her lying on the floor in Abbey's room. Taylor was crying. "She started rubbing my back," Taylor recalls. "That was a pivotal moment. I realized then that I needed to be able to find the strength to move forward, that I needed to keep Abbey part of our family, to remember the love and joy she brought to us, but for everyone else's sake, I also needed to move away from the sorrow."

For Taylor, moving away from the sorrow some days meant

simply getting out of bed and getting dressed. She told herself she had no choice but to keep moving, to keep putting one foot in front of the other. There was no other option if she ever wanted to keep living a happy life. Her next choice was to form Abbey's Hope.

"You have to make the choice to survive something like this," Taylor says. "I can promise you that after losing a child, it's a lot easier to lie in bed than it is to get up. When I launched Abbey's Hope, I chose to get up, and that—combined with my children and my husband—keeps me getting up every morning."

Today Taylor and Abbey's Hope have advocated for new national pool- and spa-safety legislation. They've also established a charitable foundation that funds the creation of public-service announcements, public swimming lessons and special water-safety education programs.

"When Abbey was first injured, I told myself that she would beat the odds, that somehow we would get past this," Taylor tells me. "When that didn't happen, when everything went wrong, I turned outside of myself and worked to help other mothers and their children. Ever since, that's been my survival strategy."

Still my baby

It was five in the morning when a police officer—accompanied by a priest—knocked on Jane's front door. She knew without asking that this early-morning visit had to do with her twenty-three-year-old son.

"They said, 'May we speak with you?'" Jane recalls. "I asked, 'Is it about Austin?' When they said yes, I asked, 'He isn't dead, is he?'"

Jane's fear was grounded in her youngest child's years-long struggle with substance abuse. Austin began drinking and smoking pot when he was in high school; by the time he was in his twenties, he had been in and out of numerous treatment facilities. His parents had tried every approach to help him beat his addictions, but as Austin moved into his twenties, they'd decided to let him go. He was an adult, after all, and they knew there was no way that they could make him turn sober if he didn't want to save himself.

"I'd relinquished him in the later part of his life," Jane tells me.

A striking woman with thick, dark hair and kind eyes, she says that it was hard to let her son go, but she and her husband Larry felt like they had run out of options. "Eventually you learn that people have to crawl out of addiction themselves," Jane continues. "We'd done tough love. I was always trying to step in there and help, but as Austin got older, I started thinking he has to do this on his own. I said, 'I've given you to God.' When Austin heard that, he'd laugh and say, 'There is no way you're ever going to be able to detach from me.'"

In a way, that was true, Jane says. She always felt a tug of worry about her son, but once she realized that she couldn't make him get better on his own, she also understood that she had been trying to live his life for him. For Jane, a deeply religious person, giving her son up to God was a true act of faith, a way of trusting that the universe had a plan for his life.

Because Austin's addiction problems ran so deeply, Jane couldn't help but worry about how his life would turn out. In the back of her mind, she always thought that he might die young. "Whenever you have a child who's suffering from addiction like Austin was, it's in the back of your mind that someday they might die, that the police will show up at your house," she says. And then it happened. "In Al-Anon, they tell you the options for addiction are recovery, insanity, or death. There's always a fear that you could get that call one day. Most parents who have children who suffer like Austin did have that fear."

In the months before he died, Austin seemed to be turning a corner, Jane tells me. Then his recovery faltered. "He was actually going to AA meetings, actually making an effort," she says. "When he died, he was on a trip to Madison. He was going to a treatment program in Hudson, Wisconsin, but at the last minute he changed his plans and went to Madison instead."

Austin planned to stay with friends in Madison, but on his first night in town he was shot and killed by a stranger during a confrontation outside a bar. The shooter, who had a previous diagnosis of mental illness, told police he was acting in self-defense and was later acquitted of Austin's murder. He served no jail time. Though many would find such emotions to be justified, Jane tells me she and her husband never felt angry with the man who killed her son. Part of that may be because Jane believes that everything that happens on earth is predesigned by God. If that is so, how can she be angry over her son's death?

"From the very beginning, Larry and I didn't have any anger against this guy who killed Austin," she says. "I was raised in a really spiritual church that was very much about forgiveness, that we are forgiven no matter what we do. You just repent and live a better life and God is merciful. That's been a constant with me."

After the acquittal, Jane and Larry continued to feel no anger. It was, Jane says, like "God had lifted that anger from us." She adds, "We didn't carry that anger. After the trial, we talked to his parents and said, 'I'm sure this has been an awful thing for you as well.' Later, in the paper, they said that Austin had probably been misrepresented and that we were nice people. They were nice people, too. Their son had schizophrenia. He had been in the Bosnian war. On another night he and Austin may have gotten along."

And Jane's not mad at God, either, for taking Austin at such a young age. "I feel like God was carrying Austin," she says. "His death was merciful. He was so sick when he died, and through his death, God helped him move to the next level, and about that I'm joyful."

If Jane's accepting response to her son's death seems unrealistic to you, you're not alone. Others have wondered if she's coping with this tragedy in a healthy way.

Jane has always been a deeply religious person; her son's tumultuous teen and young-adult years drew her even further into her faith. If a belief that her son's death is part of God's greater plan gives Jane peace and joy in this life, if she doesn't judge others who believe differently, what could be wrong with that? Losing Austin tore Jane's heart out of her body. It was a physical pain greater than anything she had ever experienced. Faith pulled her back together, and for that she's grateful.

"It was so, so horrible learning about Austin's murder," she says to me. "When I asked, 'It's about Austin, isn't it?' And they said, 'Yes.' I just fell to my knees, like I had been punched in the stomach. Everything drained out of me. Everything was gone."

But just days after Austin's death, Jane felt a quiet groundswell of strength. "I felt God filling me up and giving me strength," she says. "Part of that is shock, I suppose, but it lasted for months. I still feel it. It was like a holy anesthesia that came over me. It just stayed. God was giving me joy in my heart. Three days, a week after his death, I would have bursts of joy. Supernatural things were happening, dreams where Austin was coming to us. One morning I woke up eight days or two weeks after Austin died and I had this lightness in my heart. I looked at Larry and said, 'Let's go canoeing.' He said, 'OK.' We ran out, got the canoe." Jane and Larry live across the street from a lake. "We were carrying the canoe, and as we were crossing over to the lake, we ran into the police officer who'd come to the house to tell us Austin died," she recalls. "He looked at me and said, 'You're smiling.' I said, 'Yeah.' He said, 'It's faith, isn't it?' I said, 'It is.' I looked up and I saw there was this huge double rainbow going over the lake. I couldn't take my eyes off the rainbow. I think Larry felt the same way. I had a real lightness of spirit."

Ron Gaber, author of *The Death of Adult Children Through the Eyes of Grieving Parents* and former associate professor at A.T. Still University, says that for parents, the death of an adult child is just as traumatic as the death of a younger child. Grief cannot be measured or predicted by age, he says. For a parent, loss of a child is still devastating, no matter what the child's age.

For his book, Gaber surveyed bereaved parents of adult children. His respondents told him that they felt that outsiders often expected them to "get over" their loss quickly because their child was an independent adult at the time of their death. "One of my big discoveries was just how little support and help that these parents were receiving from friends and families," Gaber tells me, adding that such parents need as much support as bereaved parents of younger children. They also need constant acknowledgement of their loss, like cards and messages of support on significant anniversaries and holidays.

"The loss of an adult child is a terrible loss like any other loss," Gaber says. "We need to treat it that way."

Lean on me

In the days and hours after Austin's death, Jane and her husband were showered with support from friends and family, who rushed to their side to hold them up through their grief. Jane credits that love and support with helping her live beyond the tragedy of her son's untimely death. "My friends have been so awesome. They just piled into our house the day that Austin died. My family, too—they all came. It was like a love fest for three days. People just coming and huggin' and lovin'. That's huge."

And friends came forward in surprising ways, Jane says. "After Austin died, my best friend from way back—we've been soul sisters all these years—she came to me right away and she slept with me for four or five days. I couldn't sleep that well, and she stayed with me to witness my grief. It felt like God was waking me up and helping me prepare for the funeral. I had nerves of steel that day."

Jane didn't have a guidebook for how to survive this trauma. Instead, because the pain of losing her youngest child felt so raw and animalistic, she decided to let her natural instincts take over. She decided to grieve in her own way.

"I instinctively did so many things," she tells me. "When we needed to give Austin's clothes to the mortuary, I methodically ironed his underwear and oiled all of the clothes that they needed for cremation. After the funeral, I went up to a cabin in the woods with my friends. We heated up the sauna and I went in and cried my heart out. Deep inside, I knew that eventually I would be OK. The rest of my life would be like a song. It would end and I would be smiling."

Still, even though her faith gave her a peace that all would be right in the end, for Jane, grief wasn't always easy. Because the pain could be overwhelming at times, she somehow instinctively realized that she needed to gather up all the random flashes of happiness that occurred after her son's death and hold on to them for moments of great pain.

"I took all the pieces of joy that would come to me and came to me that rainbow morning," she says, reminding me of that long-ago morning canoe ride. Savoring the joy, Jane tells me, was "the only way I could survive."

Now, five years after Austin's death, Jane continues to grieve, but in a different way. Her faith remains central to her survival, and prayer is a big part of that. "I'm not a very disciplined person," Jane says. "I'm random. But I do try to sit down quietly and enter into conversation with God and say, 'Help me.'"

Jane says she also tries to incorporate a hybrid form of Eastern religious practice into this time that she calls her "grief journey."

"I have been practicing yoga-type breathing that I learned on a retreat," she says to me with a small laugh. "Since Austin's death, I try to be more intentional about breathing and relaxing. When I approach prayer I try to be relaxed, too. They say praying is talking to God—and meditation is listening to him."

While she still thinks about her son many times every day, Jane says that as the years have passed since his death, her pain has grown far less acute. She's come to a point where she now sees Austin's death as a blessing of sorts, a wrenchingly painful experience that has brought her, almost conversely, closer to God. When she was at her lowest, she says, her faith was at its strongest.

"When you are on your knees," she says to me, "it is a lot easier to believe in God."

And even from the beginning, Jane insists that when she was stuck in a dark tunnel of grief, she somehow felt she could see her way out to the other side. "Deep inside, I always felt that Austin's death was something I was going to get through," she says. "After he died, everything in the world felt a little holy to me. I felt like I wanted to be simpler. I didn't want to wear makeup. I wanted to enter my grief and go really deep into it. I knew it was going to be hard to go in, but I also knew I would come out the other end."

Comfort in chaos

Sometimes Kate feels like she didn't have time to grieve the death of her infant son Liam. At least not right away. That's because Liam was one of a set of twins. Both babies were born alive, but Liam died in the neonatal intensive care unit a few days after his birth. His twin brother Ben survived. And Kate and her husband also had an older son, Evan.

Sometimes Kate thinks she survived her newborn son's death because she was surrounded by the happy chaos of life with young children.

"My children and their needs were what kept me going through all of this," she tells me from her home in Nova Scotia, Canada. "The fact that we already had Evan and that we were bringing Ben home gave us something to work toward. When you have young children, you have to keep ticking and making grilled cheese sandwiches and getting up in the morning and playing Thomas the Tank Engine. Your son demands it. He doesn't have the pathos that we adults have in life. He doesn't have the context."

Ben and Liam suffered from a rare condition known as twin-to-twin transfusion syndrome. In this syndrome, identical twins share the same placenta, and one twin drains blood and fluid from the other. When twins with this syndrome are born, the smaller, or "donor" twin, is paler, weaker, and sicker. Liam was the donor twin. He survived the birth, but only lived for a few days before dying.

In the days leading up to Liam's death, Kate and her husband, Justin, basically lived at the hospital. They hoped against hope that both of their sons would live.

"I was wandering the halls of the hospital every day," Kate says. "I was a complete mess but I was there mucking through it. I would see the boys in there. I was always thinking to myself, 'If they have to be in there suffering through this, what I have to do is inconsequential.' I could hardly keep my eyes open. A one-pound, two-pound baby in the NICU, especially if it is yours, is horrific. They are the most pitiful things you have ever seen."

Kate has kept a blog for years, and during the twins' hospitalization, she felt compelled to write about what was happening. Getting the words out felt like a kind of therapy, she says to me. Her posts about her sons' condition were read by people from all over the world, and almost magically, she says now, she was welcomed into a community of mothers who had experienced the serious illness and death of their babies.

"The writing and the blog really saved me," Kate says. "To have other people read what I'd written, get in touch with me and say, 'You are saying things I can't articulate,' or 'I lived through this and you will, too,' helped me regain my sanity. There is this crazy intense sisterhood of women who've gone through this, and when I started writing about what was happening, they just came out of the woodwork and held my hand."

But not everyone felt like Kate's open approach to the grieving process was healthy. As her posts increased, some people who knew Kate well expressed concern that she was buried in her grief, that she was sharing more of her inner life with the world than was healthy.

"There was a point right before or right after Liam died when some people in my family were starting to get really worried about me," she says. "They were sending messages through Justin, saying, 'Kate needs to pull it together. She has other children. She has to stop writing so much in that goddamned blog. She is just wallowing.' I don't know if I've ever felt so unjustly attacked in my life."

Even though she was writing thousands upon thousands of words about Liam and his death, she had never felt more focused on the lives of her living children. After the cold shock of Liam and Ben's birth and heart-wrenching reality of Liam's eventual death, everything else in her life—including her successful career as a marketing copywriter—seemed inconsequential. All she really wanted to do was care for her two surviving sons.

And because she was driven to protect and care for Ben and Evan, Kate felt it was impossible to be smothered by grief.

"The reality of the existence of Evan and Ben helped bring us up for air," she says. "Ben would cry all night long. He didn't know that I was busy crying about his brother. And I had to get up in the morning because Evan was there, because Evan needed scrambled eggs. He was always so cheerful and running around. It rubs off on you."

There are still days when Kate wishes she'd had more time to focus on her grief over Liam. Now, years later, it's still there, though the pain has faded with time. Grief shifts, grows, and fades, Kate says. These days, she tries to acknowledge those feelings and make time for them when they resurface.

"If I feel like I need to swim in it, I swim in it," Kate says. "Sometimes I still feel like there is this little soul floating around out there that wants to be part of our family, so I'll cry and I'll write about it and cuddle with Ben and feel horrible and guilty and replay it over and let the demons in for a while. Then, after some time, I stop. As the years have gone by, it's gotten easier to set the grief aside, but it is still there. I suppose it always will be to some extent, but we are working on making it better. It is our only choice."

Pat Loder of Compassionate Friends says that her grief over the loss of her children still remains part of her life, but several years after their deaths, she made a conscious effort to move on. She had not died alongside her children, and even though this fact implanted a deep ache in her heart, she realized that if she wanted to make her remaining years of life worth living, she had to set at least some of her grief aside. There were days it felt impossible, like pushing a heavy boulder away from a cave, but she focused on the effort, and now she'd say her life is filled with joy.

"I think that sometimes bereaved people have to make a conscious effort to want to feel better again," Loder tells me. "A lot of times, I see people who want to own and wrap themselves in that grief. That is normal, especially when you're newly bereaved. But if you are going to keep living, some of that black veil will have to be pulled back, or at least turned from black to gray."

In the years since Liam's death, Kate has continued to blog, and she's never shied away from talking about her son or her experiences mourning his death. She has become deeply involved with the same network of grieving mothers that supported her immediately following Liam's death, and she truly appreciates the opportunity to provide support for other women who have experienced similar situations. Providing this kind of assistance feels therapeutic, she tells me; in fact, each time she helps another mother, she feels like she is one step closer to feeling at peace.

Compassionate Friends has a term for the strength that comes from assisting others, Loder says. "During our chapter training sessions, we always use the phrase 'Helping is healing.' When you meet someone who is so raw and their grief is so fresh, when you can stay with them to hold their hand, to provide a listening ear, and help them turn a small corner, it can actually be just as helpful to you."

Kate agrees. "If anything, this trauma has given me more compassion for the pain of other people," she tells me. "Who am I to say that what I've been through moves me up on the scale of people who deserve to be upset or sad with the world? I don't think there's any such thing. If I can help someone else, help ease their pain a little bit, I walk away feeling just that much lighter."

Kate thinks she has become a better, more caring person thanks to her late son. Sometimes people will talk about the difference between your heart being broken and your heart being broken open. Kate likes to look at it from a slightly different perspective.

"For me, the aftermath of great trauma and anguish has been more like looking through glass," she says to me slowly. "It was in the years since Liam's death, someone completely cleaned and polished the glass that I look through. Before, I didn't realize I was looking through clouded glass, but now I see I was. I'm seeing layers of things that I never knew existed, and it makes me care so much more, makes me realize just how delicate the world actually is.

"When Liam died, we felt like we were struck by lightning," Kate says. "That experience has given me new compassion for people who were struck by all sorts of lightning, and I think that makes me a far better person."

Survival tips for grieving parents from people who've been there:

+ **Helping is healing**, says Pat Loder.

"Sometimes reaching out and helping others who are going through the same pain that you have lived through is a way to help you process your own grief." Support organizations like Compassionate Friends provide opportunities for grieving parents to help one another through this amazing life challenge.

+ Jeremy Shatan advises grieving parents to remember that, **even after the death of a child, life goes on.**

"When our son Jacob died, my wife and I could've decided to freeze everything in time, to never take another step forward," he says, "but we were determined to keep living." The pair went on to have other children even while their oldest son was sick and dying. They continued to make plans for their future. "That is one of the ways we survived this trauma."

+ **Search for any scrap of good that can come from your child's death**, says Katey Taylor.

"With the creation of Abbey's Hope, I found a way to make sure that other children will not be injured in the same way that my daughter was," she says. In the wake of her daughter's death, Taylor still had many things to live for, but her foundation helped give her life an added sense of purpose and direction. "It helps me to feel like I am making the world a safer place."

+ **Ride the grief. Don't try to push it away**, Jane insists.

"Since Austin's death, when I feel sad, I let the sadness in. And when I feel joy, I also make room for the joy. Over time, my heart has had less room for sadness and more for joy. It feels like a natural process."

+ **Write it out**, Kate suggests. Writing down her emotions has been cathartic for Kate after the death of her infant. And, she stresses, the words you get out don't have to be artful.

"Sometimes, after Liam's death, I'd just sit down and bleed out words," she says. "There were times it hurt to do this, but inside I knew it was helpful for me and my healing process. And now I have a document of my emotions over my son's death. This feels like an important testament to his all-too-brief life."

Chapter 8
How Not to Survive

Like many people, I grew up with the impression that committing suicide was the ultimate failure. I didn't judge exactly, but a little part of me *did* think that people who took their own lives were incapable of mustering the courage to pull themselves out of the tar pit of depression. Then I met Annie.

When I first met Annie, she was sitting curled up quietly on a couch in my friend Sasha's living room, fingers flying effortlessly as she knit a complicated sweater. She was lovely, with long, curly dark hair and a kind smile. Annie was a newcomer to knitting group—a noisy cluster of smart, professional, boisterously opinionated women—and her friendly, quiet reserve appealed. We started talking that night, and I liked Annie right away. She was bright, perceptive, and bitingly funny—perfect friend material. By the end of the evening, we'd compared notes on our children (at the time we both had just one), talked about our families (Annie and her husband and son had recently moved back to her town and were living with her parents), and even exchanged phone numbers—making plans to meet for coffee or a walk.

Before the evening was over, I also learned an important piece of information about my new friend. While we snacked on cookies, fruit, and cheese, she told me, openly and straightforwardly, that she had bipolar disorder. She was diagnosed in her early twenties, she said, and she was doing well on medication. She appeared to be a mental-health activist, telling me that she spoke to groups and classes about her experience living with the disease and to medical students about coping with the side effects of the medications commonly used to treat it. I'd never met anyone who was quite so open about her struggle with the disease.

A few weeks later, when Annie and I met for our walk, I learned more. She told me about the manic episode—and subsequent crippling depression—that led to her diagnosis. She'd been just a few years out of college when it happened, she told me, living and working far away from home on the East Coast when her increasingly intense, irrational, and manic behavior led to an inappropriate affair, a called-off engagement, and broken hearts. When the mania faded, a massive depression washed over Annie like a tidal wave. She couldn't eat, couldn't think, could barely get out of bed. On the worst days, she told me, she lay on the floor, an inert pile of bones with unbrushed teeth and unwashed hair. In the end, Annie's younger brother had to fly out, scrape her off the floor, and bring her home to Minnesota.

What followed were intense therapy sessions and medication. "It was horrible," Annie admitted, but somehow she was able to pull herself out of the depression. Once the medications stabilized her system, Annie was able to get back to a semblance of her former life. She found a job, a boyfriend, and eventually a husband. Best of all, she gave birth to her son, a handsome, lively, smart boy who was the light of her life.

While the Annie I met was open about her struggles with mental illness, she seemed emotionally healthy and strong. Sure, she was cynical—but aren't most smart people cynical? She was also happy and magnetic and fun to be around. We spent more and more time together, talking about our lives. Because she trusted me enough to tell me about the biggest struggles in her life, and because I favor people who admit their imperfections, I liked her even more. I was happy to have made a new friend—an event that is all too rare in everyday adult life.

Annie and I were close for a few years before cracks started to show in her bright, sunny demeanor. First, her marriage fell apart, but she pulled herself together and built a life for herself and her son. By the time my second daughter was born, Annie had started a new job, and, as I watched from my distracted new-mom state, I noticed that she was changing, becoming more intense and unpredictable.

Annie got in trouble at work for random behavioral issues, developed a crush on a younger co-worker, and then, with little warning, fell in love with someone else. They got engaged. Abruptly announcing her plans to move across the country to live with her fiancé, Annie sold her car, gave away her dog, found a new school for her son. It all happened so fast that it made my head spin, but I tried to tell myself that I was just being boring, that my life was too predictable.

Then, just like it had all those years ago, Annie ran into a brick wall. Her manic behavior came to an abrupt stop when her fiancé—frightened by her irrational behavior—called off the engagement. Annie bitterly told the story one night at knitting group, and the usually noisy room grew silent as she talked about her anger, her broken heart.

In the weeks that followed, depression began to seep in around the edges of Annie's life. I could only watch as the soul-crushing sorrow that she had described on our first walk began to slowly take over her life like a dark cloud sliding over the sun. Annie fought valiantly against the depression, going to her psychiatrist, altering her medications, talking to friends and family, but the darkness still pulled her in. One morning, she dropped her son off at school, parked her car in a secluded spot, swallowed handfuls of pills, and waited to die. She almost succeeded.

This was Annie's first serious suicide attempt. She was discovered, near death, and brought to a hospital. She stayed there for weeks, working with doctors to make herself physically and emotionally healthy again. When I finally saw Annie again after the suicide attempt, she told me, flatly, about how the electroshock therapy that used to help pull her out of depression had erased many of her memories.

I hate to admit it, but it felt like my smart, loving, funny friend was gone. She seemed fragile, like a dried-up, molted exoskeleton that could easily blow away in the wind. I felt anxious around her, afraid to come too close for fear of crushing her.

If Annie's transformation was unnerving to me, one of her newer friends, imagine how it felt to people who had known her since childhood. One sunny summer afternoon, I met Flannery, one of Annie's oldest friends, for lunch near her downtown office. In many ways, Flannery reminds me of Annie. Like her friend, she is tall, slender, smart, and open, with curly dark hair and warm amber/brown eyes. As we sit down to eat, our conversation flows easily, like we've known each other for years.

Flannery tells me that Annie's first suicide attempt rattled everyone—even Annie. Though her closest friends and family members knew that she struggled with mental illness, they never thought she'd actually try to take her life. Her activism and openness about her struggle with bipolar disorder served as a kind of safety belt: If she was so determined to fight this disease, how would she ever succumb to its pull?

It's true that Annie knew all about her disease and the warning signs for suicide attempts, but when the depression completely took over, she felt powerless, like she had no other option but to end her life. Waking up in the hospital, she told Flannery that she realized she had made a horrible mistake. She told everyone she saw in those first few days that she was determined to make up for what had happened, hoping that her family and friends would forgive her for trying to leave them.

"After that first attempt, Annie told me, 'I'm so glad I survived that. I can't believe I did that,'" Flannery recalls. "She was overwhelmed by the fact that she had tried to kill herself. She was remorseful. We all just supported her, saying, 'We are so happy you're alive. What can we do to not let it get to that point again?'"

Everyone, including Annie, was determined to keep her alive at any cost.

The daily demon

Flannery has known Annie since they were children, when their families purchased neighboring summer homes. Her friend was a bright, beautiful, charming person, she tells me. "She was fun and hilarious and smart. Everyone always wanted to be around her."

During their teen years, Flannery and Annie and their siblings all got into regular teenage scrapes, but Annie always had a harder time shaking off her troubles. "I knew something was wrong in our teenage years," Flannery says. "The manic stuff was scary. As her friend, it was fun to be around her when she was intense and excitable, but sometimes her personality got really intense and scary. She wasn't herself. We knew something was going on even back then, but we had no idea what it was. I never would've labeled it as any kind of mental illness. I didn't have the vocabulary."

Annie is the third of four children but was particularly close to her younger brother, Mike. On another, rainier day, he's also taken time to meet me for lunch at a restaurant near his work. Over heaping plates of Vietnamese food, Mike tells me that he loved—and even idolized—his sister, but he also acknowledges that growing up she experienced periods of intense mood swings. At the time, these ups and downs just felt like part of his sister's personality, Mike says, but looking back on them, he now realizes that they were early signs of her disorder.

"She definitely had her ups and downs, periods where she was so funny and fun to be around and she was obviously very smart, artistic," Mike tells me, smiling at the memory. It's clear he likes to talk about his sister; he misses her, and seems happy to spend an hour talking about her. "Anne could be so funny and wry," he says. "She could be kind of mean sometimes but in a fun way. Everybody liked to be around her and be in on her jokes. She was clearly interested in life, but sometimes there were times when she was flat and just trying to get through."

Flannery tells me that she believed Annie fought to live up until the end. "She was in all the therapy groups she could be in. She read every mental-health book she could get her hands on. She did hot yoga. She went on long walks. She was willing to try anything. She'd stick with it, too. She was desperate for help. I would say she was a total fighter. When she got depressed, she couldn't fight anymore. Usually she'd rebound from the depression, but in those last couple of years she wasn't able to rebound from it."

Misunderstood

Bipolar disorder is a powerful, deadly disease, says Daniel J. Reidenberg, PSY.D., executive director of SAVE, a national suicide-prevention and education organization. Life expectancy for a woman with the disorder can be as much as fifteen years shorter than average, he says, with completed suicide occurring in 10 to 15 percent of people with the disorder.

"Fighting depression is a daily fight," he tells me, reminding me of Annie's nearly constant struggle to push away the dark cloud of the disease. "Sometimes it's an hourly fight. Sometimes for people it is a minute-to-minute fight."

Though it can be as deadly as many cancers, mental illnesses like bipolar are much more difficult to identify, isolate and treat, Reidenberg says. At this point, no technology readily exists that can identify mental illness. You can't scan a person's brain for bipolar disorder, and though medications can help a person live with the disease, they are far from perfect. In the last years of her life, Annie struggled to find a perfect medicinal balance, a pharmaceutical cocktail that could keep her depression at bay while letting her feel like a functioning human being.

"Mental illness is the most misunderstood disease of the human body," Reidenberg says. "We're not at the point yet where we can take X-rays and diagnose mental illness like we can with a broken bone." And the added complication is that mental illnesses like depression take away a person's will to live. "How did your friend 'fight' her mental illness?" he asks me, rhetorically. To have the will to fight something when your brain is telling you you'd rather die takes exceptional strength and heroism.

"People say, 'I'd rather struggle with depression than die from cancer,'" Reidenberg says. "But someone with cancer usually at least *wants* to live. They want to get better. A person with depression has little or no motivation to get better. I try to explain to people, For anybody who's had a headache, they are horrible and nobody likes them. Imagine having a migraine, the worst of your life. Take that migraine and multiply that by a hundred thousand. That's the kind of pain somebody suffers with a mental illness."

Maybe it's because I've witnessed my usually stoic husband curled up in a ball on the bathroom floor when he has been struck by a particularly vicious migraine, or because I watched as my beloved niece—after trying every medical intervention available—died painfully of cancer, but this analogy works for me. I understand that serious mental illness is not something to get over, but rather something to live with, for many people a lifelong struggle that cannot be cured or overcome.

"When depression takes hold, it wraps around your brain and it doesn't allow anything in or out," Reidenberg says. "All you feel is the depression. You become numb to everything else other than that pain. It hurts in the head, in the stomach, in the muscles. It hurts emotionally. It takes hold of you and it never lets go."

Struggle, then relief

In the end, for Annie at least, bipolar disorder was a terminal illness. Though she tried everything she could to beat the disease, on January 27, 2008, she ended her life by suicide.

People who knew Annie best say that at the end, she became increasingly powerless against the disease. It ravaged her brain and her body, tore apart her relationships, sapped her will to live.

"I do think that in her last six to eight months of life, Anne was in a dark place that you and I cannot even imagine," Mike tells me. Like many of her loved ones, as Annie's depression deepened, Mike grew increasingly worried that she might again attempt to take her life. In many ways, he felt like her death was inevitable. "When I finally got the call from my dad that she had died, I wasn't surprised."

Anne had become increasingly hard to live with, harder and harder to help, Mike says. He loved his sister profoundly, but as she fell further and further into the depths of depression, he couldn't help but feel tired of her urgent phone calls, of having to prop her up again and again, only to see her crumble and fall.

"When Anne died," Mike tells me, looking straight into my eyes, "there was a part of me with this profound sense of loss and sadness, but there was also a part of me with this sense of relief. It had become really hard to be with her. I say this as someone who loved my sister dearly and she was my idol, but it was, at the end, hard to be around her to support her. Even more than that, it was so sad for her. There was less and less of the ups when I recognized the funny, fun person, and you knew it was awful for her. Getting through the day was awful. I'm guessing dying felt like a relief for her. I'm glad she's not trying to do that anymore, really."

No matter what was going on in her mind, Annie did her best to present a strong face to the world, Flannery says. There were times when it was nearly impossible.

"She didn't want people to have to worry about her. She wanted to be normal. She wanted to be able to function like the rest of us do."

Thinking that exercise was good for fighting depression, Flannery suggested that her friend go out for walks around the neighborhood. I remember running into Annie on one of those walks. It was just months before she died. She was thin as a rail. She smiled weakly and talked in a rambling manner. She had a hard time meeting my eyes. Our conversation was stilted and awkward, far from the easy exchanges we had experienced in the past. I left feeling frustrated, confused, powerless to help her.

Flannery says that I wasn't the only one of Annie's friends who felt this way. "She got to the point where she was really embarrassed about existing, so walking in the neighborhood was hard. She had this horrible phobia of engaging with people. She got very reclusive in the end. A lot of people that knew her really well said, 'I didn't talk to her for a whole year before she died.'"

There came a point where her friend's end was inevitable, Flannery believes, and she thinks this reality is what so many people were reacting to when they saw her near the end of her life. The end was staring them in the face, and they felt like they needed to look away.

"My husband is a doctor," Flannery says. "When I got the call that she died, and I was screaming on the floor, he said, 'This is how people who have bipolar die. This is the end of the disease. This is how it happens and it usually happens right around this age. We could see it was coming. She'd tried once before. She tried to get herself back together. We all feel bad for her son and her family, but finally Annie's life has come to its conclusion.'"

Flannery pauses. Her next words are hard. "This death was the right timing for her," she continues. "It wasn't the right timing for anybody else. But for Annie it was the right timing. She was so depressed for so long, like two and a half years, and she couldn't think of any way she could keep living with it. I think she saw her disease as spiraling downward. It was only going to get worse."

After his sister died, Mike tells me that some mourners attempted to reassure him that he did all he could to help her. These well-wishers didn't want him to feel guilty about his sister's death, Mike says, but the truth is he never did feel guilty. Not once.

"Anne was on this really difficult, long trajectory of profound magnitude and suffering," he says. "It was horrible and sad and I still have a really profound sense of loss. No one knows you like your sibling." This statement feels particularly moving, because to me Mike looks and sounds so much like his sister. He continues, "Anne's death was a mix of complicated emotions for me. Part of this was this sense of relief. Part of that relief was mine, like this ordeal of trying to keep her propped up for so many years was finally done. Then part of that relief was for her, like her ordeal—which was way, way, way worse than mine—was finally over."

No matter how Annie's life ended, Flannery always thought of her friend as a fighter. Despite the terrible blows bipolar disorder dealt her, she kept working to regain her health. Annie was an extraordinary ordinary person, a woman who recognized her imperfections but tried to work within them with humor and good will. In the end, depression outmaneuvered her, overwhelming her defenses even as she tried in every way she could to overcome its pull.

"I think mental health really strips you of your resiliency because you are battling something that you don't have any control over," Flannery says. "Annie was an extremely resilient person from the time she was twenty when she had serious depression issues. She had to work hard to get out of bed when she was depressed, and when she was manic she had to work hard to stay in control and maintain her job. As she got older and closer to the end of her life, she started having these horrible nightmares. She never was free of this disease."

And as for my childhood belief that suicide is a coward's ending, Reidenberg tells me that the innate human impulse for self-preservation is actually so strong that it takes enormous strength of will for a person to end her own life.

"You have to know that the act of suicide actually takes a lot of courage," Reidenberg says. "The body and mind are not designed to take themselves out. It's a hard thing to do. There's ambivalence up to the moment of death. Really these are very courageous people fighting against their own will and nature."

Instead of thinking that Annie gave up on life, Flannery takes a different approach. She believes that up until the end of her life, her friend did all she could to stay alive. She was a fighter. She also believes that Annie's deep and enduring love for her son kept her alive until she decided that he'd have a better life without her. She wanted him to have a happy, normal childhood, and she felt she couldn't provide that for him anymore. "In the end, she just wasn't herself," Flannery says. "She was a different person, out of her mind with grief and desperation."

Mike delivered a eulogy at his sister's funeral. "Anne was my sister," he read to the assembled group of friends and family. "She was also my friend and among the most formative influences in my life. Like all of us, Anne was imperfect. She was complicated. She was beautiful and she was exceptionally interesting."

That complicated, interesting part of Anne's personality was what drew so many people to her, Mike believes, and in the end, the illness that magnified her complicated, interesting personality was also what killed her. For nearly forty years, Anne lived her life with an illness that slowly took her over, body and soul.

"I really do think people think of suicide as some sort of failure or failed ending, but that is not how I looked at my sister's death," Mike says. "It was jarring to me to hear people suggest that she made this sudden choice in one day. It was a lifetime in the making."

Afterword
How I Survived

Moving pictures

Earlier in my life, I decided that even though photographs can be wonderful, some moments are just too important to capture in a picture.

So instead of whipping out my camera and snapping away at every significant life event, I trained myself to take a mental picture instead, to absorb important moments, to soak in the images, sensations, sounds, and smells that I wanted to store away forever.

One example: That slow bus ride I took during a college trip to China. As we passed a tall, white apartment building, I saw an upper-floor window open and a small hand toss out one red ball. The ball seemed to drift slowly, weightlessly to the ground before landing in the green, green grass.

Or there are my children's births. The intense buildup to the sudden moment when, with one strong final push, they were born, their warm, slippery bodies finally in my arms, unfamiliar yet somehow deeply familiar.

These are pleasant images that I have replayed countless times. Recalling them is almost like opening a worn photo album and running my fingers gently over the pages. I've also recorded my share of unpleasant memories, but my personal collection tended to lean heavily toward the positive. What I wanted to recall were the things that brought me the most joy.

Then I decided to write this book.

I've been a journalist for more than two decades, so I've heard—and described in words—plenty of tough stories. And I know all about objectivity, about making the story about my sources, not about me. I do a good job at that, usually, but during the months I spent working on this book, there were times when I felt as if I'd been sucked into the vortex of my subjects' lives, recalling the crushing pain of the grieving parent or the depressing disorientation of life with a malfunctioning heart. (See my false-alarm "heart attack" at the beginning of chapter one, for instance.)

The people I interviewed for this book were all open and forthcoming, willing to recount some of the most painful moments they have ever experienced. And though I didn't actually witness any of the traumatic events they shared with me, my sense of empathy kicked in, and as I worked on the book, transcribing hours of interviews and writing down the stories, a vivid collection of my subjects' experiences began to pile up in my brain.

And then my own life—and the lives of my loved ones—took a surprising turn. Within a span of months my beloved father-in-law and niece both fell ill and died. I was with both of them just hours before they passed, and the memories of that sacred time will remain with me forever. Thinking about their deaths still makes me feel hollowed out and sad. Those they left behind continue to struggle to come to peace with the reality of their untimely exits.

In the muddle of my own grief there were days when working on the book left me depleted and exhausted. But as I continued to transcribe interviews and write, something unexpected happened: As I replayed the stories I'd collected during my research and writing, a sense of peace began to seep into the cracks of my life. My subjects' honest accounts of how they imperfectly yet bravely faced down life-shifting events were both awe-inspiring and comforting. These were real people who found that they could thrive despite major traumas. If they could do it, then so could I. I'm no Pollyanna. Reading other people's stories didn't bring me out of these experiences feeling instantly "healed," or anything like that, but knowing the stories of other people's struggles and survival made me feel like my own struggles were somehow surmountable.

And that was the reason I wrote this book in the first place. I wanted to help other people find a way through their own traumas by reading about the coping skills of others. When I experienced my own traumatic events, my subjects' stories had the effect I was hoping for. I felt less alone.

Sure, life could be easier if we could just sail through it, free of struggle or sadness. Like most people, that's the kind of life I once hoped for. And there's still a part of me that wishes that life for my daughters. But I know that an unblemished life is incomplete.

I recently came across a quote from Elisabeth Kubler-Ross, author of *On Death and Dying:* "The most beautiful people we have known are those who have known defeat, known suffering, known loss, and have found their way out of the depths. Beautiful people do not just happen." I love that sentiment because it says what I've believed for years: The most compassionate people are those who've struggled.

A good example is my own mother, a small, strong woman who survived a wartime childhood in England during the 1940s. As her relatives were bombed out of Bath, Bristol, and London, they all moved to Oxford to live with my mother, her two sisters, and their parents in their small row house. My mom ate meager portions of rationed food, gave up her bed to her grandmother and aunt, and slept on a series of cots and couches. She remembers a childhood of air raids and gas masks, of listening anxiously for the ominous "putt-putt" sound of buzz bombs. Still, she survived it all to become a gentle, gracious woman, welcoming and kind to everyone who came through her door.

Even today, as her eyesight fades and she struggles with the painful reality of my ninety-one-year-old father's advancing dementia, my mother continues to find great joy in nature, in the presence of her children and grandchildren, and the comforting rhythm of her favorite poetry.

My mom has always been particularly fond of *The Velveteen Rabbit,* a children's story in which a once plush stuffed toy becomes real only after having his whiskers loved off. She read it to me when I was a child. Later, when I was in college, I gave a copy to the man who would one day become my husband. The message? It's simple, and it's one I relearned while struggling in the tangle of writing this book: Life, while it can be filled with joyful moments, can also wear us down. But that's what makes us beautiful—and real.